Restraint

PJ Bayliss

Other titles by PJ Bayliss

Available at www.Amazon.com

Burnt (Paperback/Kindle)
ASIN: B00ID2SY3M
ISBN: 978-0473-26891-6

Absence (Paperback/Kindle)
ASIN: B00LNCO4L0
ISBN: 978-0-994-1090-19

Arriving soon

Chemical Romance series:
+ LIBRIUM +
+ CONCEPTION +
+ DELIRIUM +
+ DECEPTION +

First published 2014

1 2 3 4 5 6 7 8 9

This is a work of fiction.
Names, characters, places, and incidents are either the product of the author's imagination or are used fictitiously, and any resemblance to actual persons, living or dead, business establishments, events, or locales is entirely coincidental.

ISBN: 978-0-9941090-0-2

www.pjbayliss.com

DEDICATION

To the darkest shadows that surround me,
and in loving memory of Colin, Liz, and Chad.

CONTENTS

POETRY

ACKNOWLEDGMENTS

I wish to thank my immediate family for their patience and understanding while I wrote this book. I would never had been able to complete this work without you, and for this I am eternally grateful.

Thank you Richard, Pam, Roger, Mike, and Steven for all the discussions we had. Through your understanding, I learnt more about myself than I ever thought possible.

Thanks to the "original few" Facebook peeps who were there from day one. It was a complete blast, but sadly needed to end for the sanity of all. You will always be there with me in my heart & I am forever grateful for the laughter, inspiration, and kindness you gifted me.

PREFACE

Have you ever woken up in a cold sweat with your subconscious mind dreading the upcoming daily routine? Do you dread the regular beat of preparing for work, preening yourself in the misty mirror before disembarking as quick as you can to beat the morning traffic, only to find yourself sitting idly among hoards of commuters upon congested highways?

Your days are then filled with uneventful highlights from your work environment. Superficial "wins" conducted behind closed doors accompanied by porcelain smiles and gratuitous agreements. The working day is fulfilled through a handful of minutes, and before you know it, you're slowing grinding your way back home with the masses; where you are bound to update your spouse on the latest developments with your work colleagues.

Then, in a flashing moment, the weekend passes by, and you're briefly released from the restraint of working life. Birds suddenly find their voices in the morning, the sunbeams finally soak through your clothing and the sweet nectar of coffee magically transforms to help you relax for the day. You're finally able to spend time with those you've committed your life to and to enjoy sunsets with the family on the outdoor porch rather than with countless strangers on the commute back home.

And all too soon, you wake up once again, and the poetic restraint of life kicks in…

But what if one day, your inner conscious finally awakens, and you decide to write a note in that misty mirror for your lover to discover when she gets up? What if the voice you silenced for so many years is suddenly heard and takes center stage in your life? What if it shuts down every other element in your life, removes your sight, ability to comfortably breathe, and fills you with a mind-numbing concoction of passion, ambition, drive, and emotion?

What if you finally realize that your restraint can ultimately set you free?

SEA OF PAIN

Drifting upon scathing sea of desolate names,
The hungry, scared, barren, and enslaved,
I wade into water to depth of my knee,
To be flogged, chastised, beckoned to heed.

Amongst casual chatter the darkest evil lurked,
Identifying victims & how the red room worked,
Master's voice boomed like a heavy bass drum,
Naked bodies writhing with fluid emotion.

From shoreline I realized what had to be done,
And I unraveled the fragility of this kingdom,
In guise I approached as Eve not as Adam,
To be hustled, & accosted by angels of Satan.

I was but Titan under cover of the still night,
Spellbound maidens merely sought lust's delight,
Foul Master objected to my verse that lingered,
He eradicated all men with one tap from his finger.

The protector was vanquished, hung out to dry,
A poor child stood brave with tears in her eye,
To the sea of pain I returned once again,
Salvaging souls before they were abandoned.

A revelation of love & praise from the roses,
Lifted thy swift sword to swing down with prose,
Now the toxic sea recedes to its end,
While I'm immersed,
Triumphant,
With true friends.

BIRDSONG

The desolate rain fades away to rinse dilated black glare,
Illuminated within the night,
I sensed her,
Standing there.

I envision.
Imagine,
My numb mind gathers more,
My fantasy: Divinity, shackled, and sensual receipt in the raw.

As softly she spoke, barely noticing me bare,
From sweet dream I woke, "Comply me my Dear"
I resign myself. Leniently we touch, connect & then merge,
My fingers running softly across her refined verge.

With strengthening blood, I reduce my space,
Grasping, commanding to hasten our pace,
Slowly I withdraw …caressing shoulder & neck,
Now filled with lust, firmly hauling her back.

We writhe, intertwine, and locking ourselves in,
Drawing the exotic nectar out from her delicate sin,
The ponderous rain ceases to pour outside,
Winds collapsing to a silent sigh.

I embrace her misty shoulder as my soul pours her desert dry,
She grasps for restitution & gives out a small hollow cry,
Across distant cold breeze, birdsong echoes from the trees,
Together, gradually wilting, like fallen leaves.

She whispers my name… I love you

…Mon Ami.

PERFECT NIGHT

Amidst the dark night ahead,
My heart skips a beat,
And dreams turn wild,
For a stranger I met.

He dominates my lust,
And churns up a storm,
Capsizing inner goddess,
Overflowing with warmth.

His true intention is clear,
For love to embrace me,
Hence I listen all night,
To call his name.

Mon Ami.

ANGEL BY SURPRISE

As we danced throughout the night,
Our timing never was quite right,
Carefully waltzing upon misty deck,
Slowly to prevent fatal shipwreck.

We smiled and laughed as we immersed in fun,
She was soaked and now glistened in the hot sun,
When I mentioned that we had already once met,
She chuckled and challenged me "Wanna bet?"

Reincarnated from hot pyre of a memory past,
From a time of lost love and fires of passion last,
Tears from our eyes as the smoke blew a haze,
Overjoyed to be reunited after all of these days.

A sparkling gaze deep within blue-grey eye,
I had taken destiny's Angel by surprise.

LOVER'S LULLABY

How I cherish this time of the day,
When my lover passes by. That gleam in her eye,
Letting me know, her intention is true,
And now it is time to play.

Like smoke she lingers before me,
With a single pass. Her innocent essence. I gasp,
Trawling her night shadow behind,
She encapsulates me.

Transcending into her watery depth,
From heel to toe, bended knee to divine luxury,
Encapsulating her majestic body within,
I submit, gently washing her silk cortex.

Emerging from heated pool, she begins to sway,
I surge & break fall. We land ourselves, upon cold wall,
Our eyes never depart from each other,
Her cheeky grin implies I must stay.

She grasps hold during our slow rise,
My shoulders clench taut, thighs clasp tight in embrace,
Her feet heave up from the ground,
I vow never to release her firm vice.

Together we dance as one,
Biting kiss upon neck, she wraps arms, we've begun,
My girth ruptures as she is splayed astride,
Silently she moans, "…Make love to me Hun."

I gently place her up & away,
Upon leather-clad pad, strapped to chains, haven above,
I release her to caress, loves motion applies the rest,
I whisper "…Sway Baby, Sway".

Hair thrown back upon breeze,
Lover's delight, steam rising upon sight,
Upon departure & re-entry, she continues to glisten,
Her first luxury comes with ease.

I raise my jilted lover's head,
Forsaken she submits to my hunger & intent,
I cast & expose my maiden down,
Caressing her wounds upon bed.

I am now captured by my own prey,
Arched back, penetrated and interlocked by firm thigh,
She motions to submerge my soul deep within,
Together we sing lullaby.

"…Sway baby, Sway".

MASTER

What is a MASTER?
But a mere soul drafted upon string,
Like a toy wooden puppet,
Vacant of finger ring,
Hung.

His limb,
Mind,
Tongue, and heart,
Strung so tight,
Could they rip him apart?

Lines so taut. Poised delicately between sublime souls,
Faith. Belief that a subtle tug, would lead ONE to fold,
Inclinations to snap, stretch, or fall apart,
Potentially, rupture of heart.

Gifted knowledge.
MASTER cannot dictate or command ONE to submit,
From torn earth, they must gift him the right.

Remit,
One must provide desire to tension his bow,
To thrive, Love,
To & fro.

The MASTER must first give to earn trust,
Respect space,
Never feign,
In order for ONE to willingly submit,
Call out his name.

Her echoes must not drift or outcry false lust,
It must be spoken,
As a whisper of love.

KISS - HER

As our eyes met, my waters stirred & my internal goddess moaned for release to splay open and to encapsulate his hardness. His fingers met mine, intertwined slowly he lifted me from where I sat and placed the champagne glass down onto the table. Together we stood and embraced the morning sun, with a snap my blouse fell to the floor and his gentle smile turned into a smirk.

I was now revealed naked before his presence. Goddess wept a tear as his hand firmly grasped my buttocks while his other hand caressed the back of my neck. I closed my eyes signaling him entry & what seemed a lifetime of breathlessness.

He sealed my delicate lips, his warm steaming breath penetrating every internal inch of my body and soul. My feelings of abandonment and emotional desire were now swirling with wanton lust and need for him to penetrate me further like never before.

His gracious tongue teasingly touched and tasted my own edging me further into an unknown path of ecstasy. I had to accept this man and his mysterious past into my life at whatever cost.

We parted, with barely a movement of eye we knew, his bedroom was where I would be taken: the only sanctum where we could be within each other and freed from this grey world.

KISS - HIM

This moment had slipped upon us, now it was our fraction of time. She departed from bath, adorned gown, stood in the shade of silk & lace. She longed for my deep embrace.

Her dilation opened deep soul, the waters stirring. From my vantage point, I caught whisper of inner goddess's sigh as she splayed to encapsulate me. Our fingers met, intertwined slowly as I bore down to carry her away. With sharp thrust, the slender glass shattered but we continued to embrace in the morning sun.

A gentle snap. Her blouse fell to ground as my smile turned into smirk.

She was now revealed naked before me as her goddess wept a tear. With one hand firmly grasping her buttocks my other hand caressed the back of her neck. She closed her eyes signaling me entry in what seemed a lifetime of breathlessness.

I sealed her delicate lips, my warm steaming breath penetrating every internal inch of her body and soul. My gracious tongue teasingly touched and tasted hers. We edged further into an unknown path of passionate ecstasy. Feelings of abandonment and emotional desire were now swirling with wanton lust and need. She whispered for me intrude and penetrate further like never before.

Our lips parted with barely a movement of eye. She knew my bedroom was where I would take her: the only sanctum where we could be within each other and freed from this grey world.

BREATHLESS

I consume twisted winds from your soul,
To retrieve cruel love from aching hole,
I accept poisoned and twisted past,
Invoking true love that forever lasts.

As we have been cheated by dimension & time,
For now we connect and our bells toll in chime,
Each dusk & dawn enlightens common path,
Nothing shall stop us from falling in love.

Once paths meet there is nothing within,
Prompting any famine of a banquet of sin,
As I gasp from your kiss my world grows heady,
Your scented haven awash from lust's eddy.

Amidst my panting you grapple my hair,
Entrusting my growl into your flaming lair,
Bursts of emotion lapping at my Cupid's lip,
Currents of love potion I eagerly sip.

Gulping for air my heart starts to flutter,
As you melt before me like warm butter,
Tongue dipping and diving as you flood,
Flame flickering from igniting rosebud.

Goddess breaks away now she's woken,
Moaning with desire, dam is broken,
Torrents of nectar cascade down my face,
I become intoxicated through your embrace.

Upon foot or steed, in shining armor,
I yearn to rest ship in your safe harbor,
By minute we whittle down life's sour zest,
Until I once again shall become breathless.

FLOGGER OF DEATH

Strapping on tainted leather glove,
My mighty flogger is then charged,
Her deep lusty throaty growl,
Echoes across the land.

My flogger ripped through her white flesh,
Spilling a speck of pink,
Gnawing away with determined desire.

As I sliced down through her V,
She resisted abruptly,
I applied,
Flogger tried, patiently.

With undeniable force she gave,
And then breached,
My sanctuary held fast,
Head rushing, I almost passed.

With force constant applied,
Her advance was denied,
Head blood in retreat,
She lay, submitted at my feet.

BREATHING

Amid midnight's gentle ticking,
My dull heart keeps on beating,
Moonlight beams are trickling,
His deep voice is my greeting.

My passion surges rising,
His arms strong & embracing,
I set sail upon his horizon,
Dull heartbeat turn to racing.

Our eyes glance & remain starring,
Back arches towards rearing,
Deep heat inside me seething,
Until rest completed, we are breathing.

PITCH BLACK SLAVE

Down incline I stride,
I am so terrified inside,
The toxic fog resides,
Inside thy skull's hide.

At rock bottom, Snap,
A violent crack,
White flesh turns black,
Red topples from stack.

A whisper and crook,
Fluttering leaves of books,
Pitch soul, seeping brook,
Somber, petrified look.

Lost luminescence,
My immortal essence,
Hacked open crescent,
Interred thy peasant.

Strained gas mask hides,
My deep burning inside,
Passionate desire,
Pitch cast on pyre.

Red ooze is freed,
Amidst fog I breathe,
Revelation, can it be,
My discovered entity.

Wading from surf,
Of red afterbirth,
Soaked to my girth,
I scour this earth.

I choose not to reveal,
I will not cut peal,
Pitch can't up keel,
I must begin heal.

I pause and grin,
I breathe from within,
A shiver ignites sin,
Static crawls across skin.

I relax face,
Provide them space,
We heal within grace,
Within our small place.

Release I could,
Trust I surely would,
Our love is so good,
As they knew it would.

Welded as friends,
Pitch journey ends,
Tight gas mask blends,
Writing entity mends.

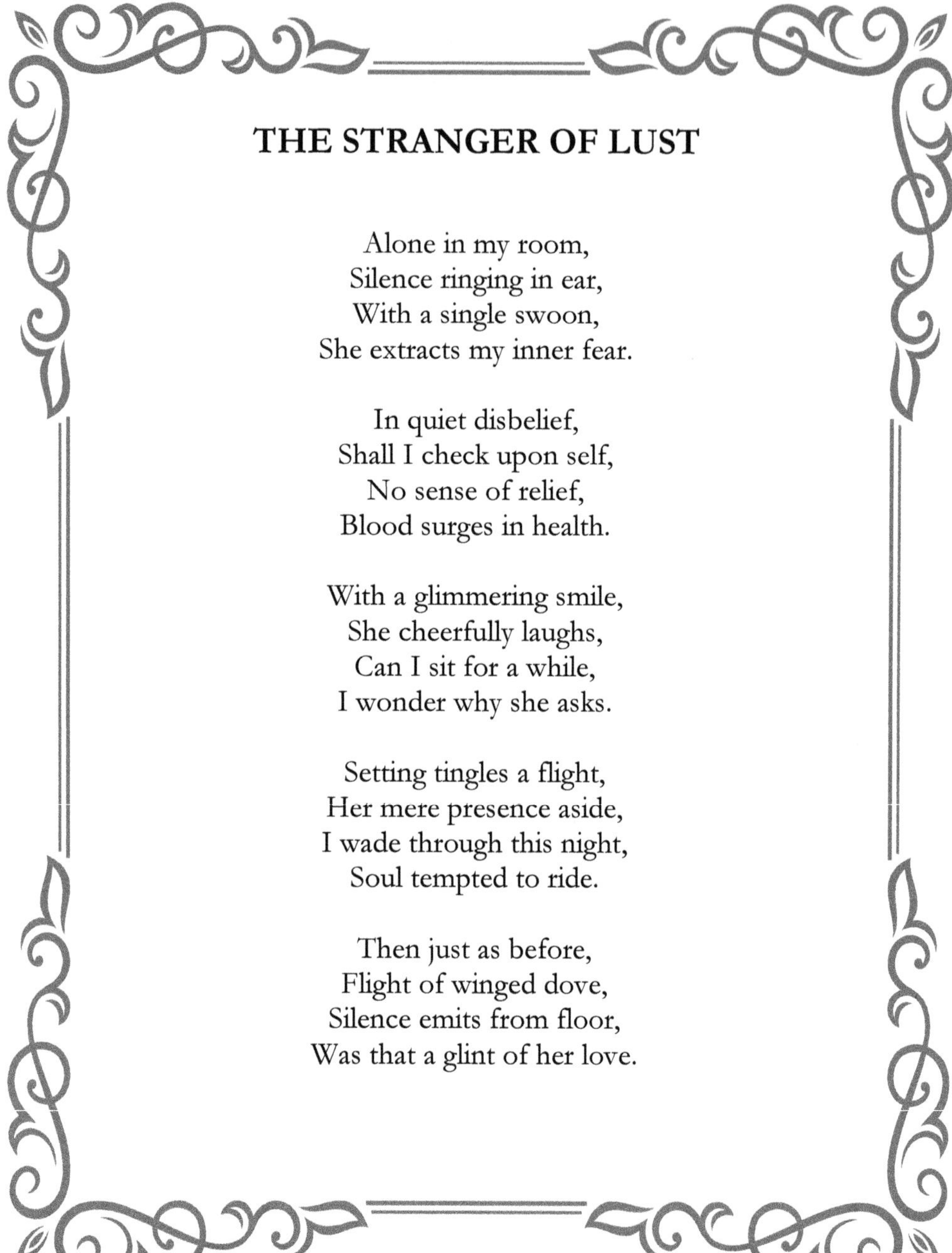

THE STRANGER OF LUST

Alone in my room,
Silence ringing in ear,
With a single swoon,
She extracts my inner fear.

In quiet disbelief,
Shall I check upon self,
No sense of relief,
Blood surges in health.

With a glimmering smile,
She cheerfully laughs,
Can I sit for a while,
I wonder why she asks.

Setting tingles a flight,
Her mere presence aside,
I wade through this night,
Soul tempted to ride.

Then just as before,
Flight of winged dove,
Silence emits from floor,
Was that a glint of her love.

LOST LOVE

I once lost you my friend,
You were hidden deep,
I thought this was the end,
'Til smirk on my face you crept.

From within my blank stare,
Eyes glazed for many miles,
Black pupils, as I wasn't there,
As lips turned into smile.

Friend, you insisted from beneath,
Now aching to be let past,
My clenched grip & white teeth,
Your presence heard as a laugh.

Rushing out from my throat,
While my belly starts to rumble,
Those around me almost gloat,
As you break pace into a chuckle.

Tingling sensation over me,
As a dance, skip & jiggle,
This visit has been welcomed,
My dear friend, contagious giggle.

DESIRE TO RESTRAIN

Two souls bound together,
Withheld a world apart,
No leather strap or tether,
Yet, a single tear from the smart.

Two streams flowing to a river,
Gently trickling away,
Eroding with tantric shiver,
Silently cutting the glacier away.

Two clocks quietly ticking past,
Arms never in the same place,
Souls that bond, strengthening fast,
Fused closer still upon meeting face.

Two birds. One needs to take flight,
Rare songbird edges from stale nest,
Flightless avian forages at ground height,
Quietly chirping. Shall do my very best.

Two eyes gazing through the damp fog,
Endless smile that catches the sun,
Fearless avian emerges from log,
Curiosity. Need an assist Hun?

Two distant views of desired life,
Separate, yet each is the same,
Emptiness, torture, sorrow & strife,
Fates destiny on either plane.

Two voices echo through thick forest,
So many prints with curious clicks,
Drifting between, amour's mist,
Restrained flight, wings clipped.

Two era-torn lovers cast into a spell,
Absence in time bonding stronger still,
Each plans to escape their own private hell,
Desire to restrain, at sublime free will.

TWISTED SPLICE

The toxic portal beckons as I sleep,
Homage to restless voices that I keep,
Blue drug induced cover slides away,
Revealing yet another fucking day.

The plane of light levitates above,
Gliding past like a silent dove,
Ticks of time pounding my head,
Blackened eyes streaked bloodied red.

Playful demons pulsating under skin,
Spiritual nuance constrains passage in,
Residing passengers are very agitated,
His expressions erupt as now aggravated.

Tailored cloth embellish flesh color,
We survive dreary days after each other,
Should I not disturb the transit air,
My breath would forever linger there.

Sacrificial souls shuffle upon granite,
Tireless hours burnt to save dead planet,
Steel chambers humble the crowds,
Praise & reward to the plundering proud.

Whatever happened to the leading unique?
Those whom care or protect those who seek,
Success defined: a collection of embossed card,
And custom tailored cloth to hide rich lard.

Dare not perceive me as fallen from peak,
As I rise from my cast shadow as unique,
Nor is my imprudent mind a twisted grain,
Barren soul rinsed by foaming sea of pain.

The dawn, dusk, and space in between,
No longer offer any veracious meaning,
Now I find comfort with pumping rose,
To form stream of Black n White prose.

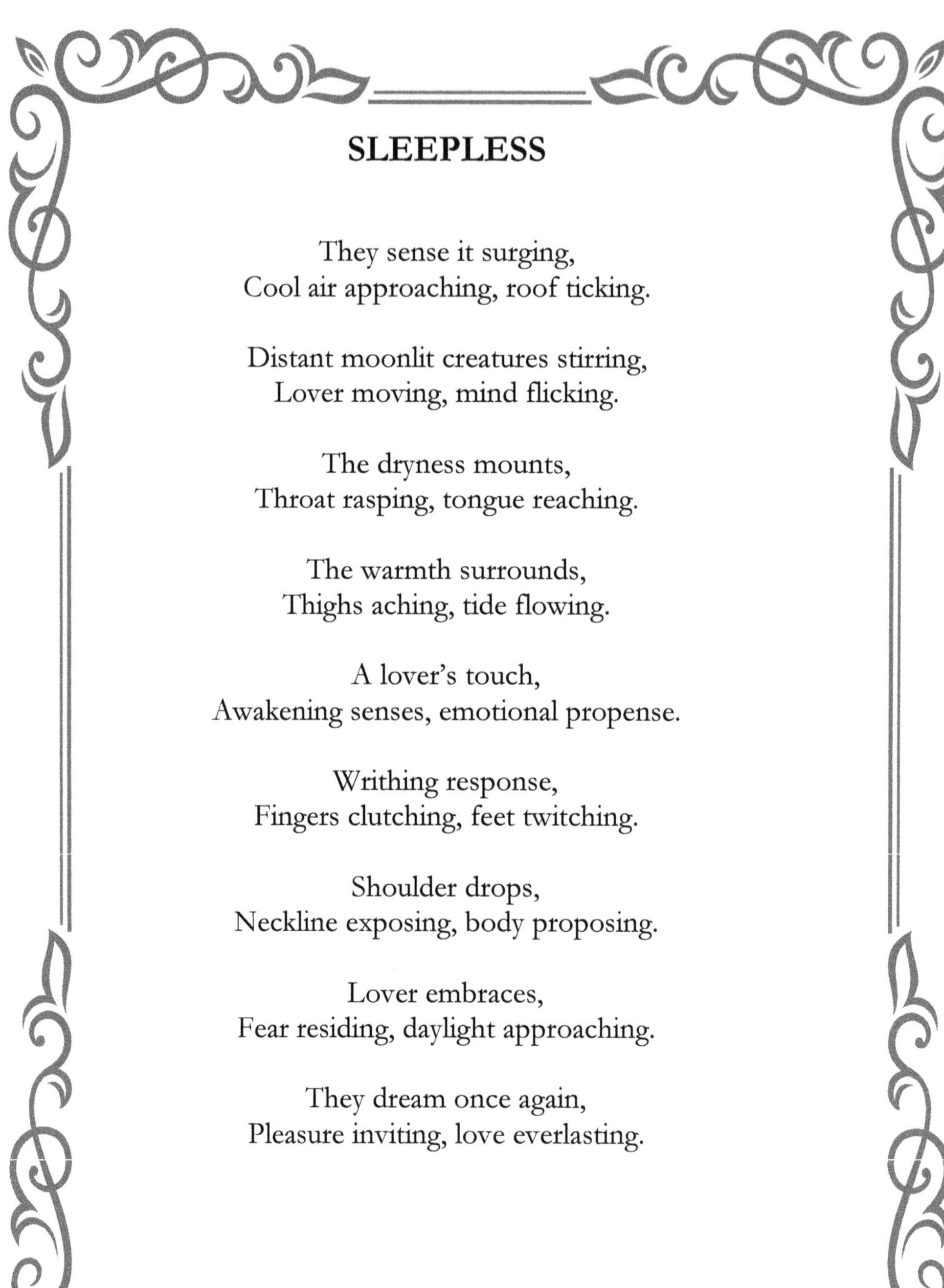

SLEEPLESS

They sense it surging,
Cool air approaching, roof ticking.

Distant moonlit creatures stirring,
Lover moving, mind flicking.

The dryness mounts,
Throat rasping, tongue reaching.

The warmth surrounds,
Thighs aching, tide flowing.

A lover's touch,
Awakening senses, emotional propense.

Writhing response,
Fingers clutching, feet twitching.

Shoulder drops,
Neckline exposing, body proposing.

Lover embraces,
Fear residing, daylight approaching.

They dream once again,
Pleasure inviting, love everlasting.

SLAVE POET

Lips sealed upon command as he motions towards his mast,
Threaded hair though fingers while his golden prose starts to cast.

Words whispered in midnight air she casts off inner doubt & fear,
Morning my love, I know you may, flog my aching sorrow bare.

Slowly she rolls upon firm bed revealing herself to his deep mind,
Agonizing dreams, leaving head, striking upon his words so kind.

Linen sheets cast over chamber as eyes shut, tremble, cast to release,
Searching for a love, as never before, reaching inside seeking inner peace.

Together they weave golden embrace rhythmically writing upon blank page,
Willing to oblige at his last pace while loving together through a lost age.

Cast to his spell they seek new height, her feet cast astride for morning relief,
Steadfast working waters of doubt, stroking the slave poet beyond belief.

His hand reaches forth to silky hair, surrendering, she opens wide to glory,
Hot lava soaks lips, mouth, & throat as she impulsively bursts into his story.

LUST'S FIRST TOUCH

I recall my first touch, but barely the next,
Life after that is a just black & white mess,
Crisp romance and desire is a climatic blast,
Lust-filled longing to grapple with Goddess's clasp.

Toes thrust through the sand as surf spills over feet,
Emotionless shadows resign and copulate in defeat,
Transfixed entanglement with tightening embrace,
Heavenly scented mist of Venus in my face.

The pink surge commences from bosom to torso,
Rush of engorged blood. Palms, cheeks, & neck also,
Burst of pupil dilation as we gaze eye to eye,
Blurt of your submission seeps across thigh.

Vigorously working resolute solution away,
Silently screaming and beckoning to flay,
Amphitrite's wash breaks loose and soaks deep,
Mournful crying of climax as together we peak.

Subdued we release with shuddering spasm,
As I fully explore depths of your sacred chasm,
A glimmer of passion as we silently suspend,
Adorning a look of love I wish will never end.

LUST'S NEXT TOUCH

Our worlds no longer combine,
Colliding they are separated by time,
'Til I'm left with a postcard of sun tarnished image,
Of early days when we both looked so fine.

First love sang with a chorus so sweet,
Sandaled in uniform. Brown hair capturing the breeze,
Her smile transferred to me through a single kiss,
My entire world stood still whenever she appeared.

Years of playful canter and fun,
She was my idol who owned my very soul,
Until that fateful evening she left me,
I was cast forever spinning into love's deepest of holes.

Emerging I clawed away at any light,
Freed at last seemed to have a certain appeal,
Blending into the group. Bleeding brought under control,
I was quite happy to destroy any new seal.

Society never allowed me to fit,
Top of the wanted list. Considered as best of friend,
One who could talk, be there or be in there,
My induction into lust seemed never to end.

With lust came romance, or so I thought,
Devoid of self-conscious I dug myself in so deep,
From bended knee to giving my last ounce of soul away,
Countless cycles before she finally seeped.

My mind parted like a comet in the sky,
Awash of the waters from the beautiful nest,
Now I weep every time I remember,
A lifetime of never ever proving to be her best.

Shut the whole thing down,
Let the mist move in and take total control,
Man the mainsail and drift away,
Barren boy can never swim in that bowl.

I wished for the day we would touch again,
Her silk skin so pure, gentle & fine,
My exterior is weathered & worn,
Her absence of touch has neither healed, nor sealed thee.

Thus my brittle heart is now easily torn,
Exposed, once again, like my first romance,
Leaves me poised to fall. To love & to be loved again,
However, where the wind takes me, may not be where I land.

REALIZE

As the glassy glare from lover's face ripped like hunger through my flesh,
I was condemned to depth of forbidden lake and forced to rise from bondage,
Remorsefully I sunk into the pitch-black pool in vow of silence,
My hunger for passion gnawing away with every batch from my appendage.

As chilling echoes of distant love haunted resolute hills and valleys,
Pasture turned to dust underfoot as I begged to wade among her seepage,
My outlawed soul surfaced for air, absent mind was lost and vanquished,
Upon sight of light from broken pond, my mind stretched like a bridge.

Lust of sin gushed in torrent to rupture my white skull into half,
Mournfully I shrivel and cried within the chilling absence of lover's embrace,
Her ebb and flow no longer drifts inside me with peaceful harmony or pace,
Forcefully my hand reaches down to key and unlatch my mourning hostage.

With tear creeping from eye,
I realize,
I would have preferred it if she had killed me.

HOLD ME

I'm drifting away,
Amidst subtle hues of dove grey,
Weighed down by the deep,
I sink to where I now lay.

You cut me some slack,
As I leave and turn back,
My soul fading to pitch black,
As does my final act.

I surrender to despair,
The pyre flares without warn,
Yet your silence in morn,
Dulls even the brightest of dawn.

So my new journey begins,
Washed pure from prior sin,
As within this tense grin,
Lies a shadow cast from rusty tin.

I may have your sight,
Without soft touch from your light,
I spread wing in silent flight,
And bid for what was once our sight.

Thus, torment lies inside,
Releasing salted dew known as tears,
As my weary dry hide cracks,
Spilling out from within to rid my fear.

Forced refugee from the night,
I sleep now when we once might,
I place my total amount,
As I will soar towards my own sight.

Breathing air from the past,
I scroll for those who accept me,
Drawing in deep sole of passion,
You no longer try to hold me.

AFTERCARE

There is an urge to explain various welts and pain,
As they were wrapped in darkness, pity, and vain,
Separated, I sit, and quietly reside beside myself,
Through black holes I peered, drained of inner health,
I cannot exist as one without living the other,
Poetic voices within propel an ice-cold shudder.

I told him.
He listened.

Red swirl in his brain broke over the levy,
Eyes wide open he could not see it was me,
So he bore down on my hide with great force,
My resilience was too weak, drained of course,
He passed over his liquid as if it was wine,
I admitted that this scene was my first time.

I questioned.
He answered.

The pair of us sat humbly in the sun,
With myself beside me, still joined as one,
Separated only by fragile panes of glass,
I eased into a comfortable pace at last,
The surrounding fog had begun to chill,
Tension released to welcome the thrill.

He commanded.
I complied.

The fog now removed from within my eyes,
I caught my own truth, to my own surprise,
I had not brutally torn myself apart,
It was just a mere fault of my aching heart,
He revealed his own love waiting quietly near,
How history split apart what they now share.

He scorned me.
I already knew.

RETURN

Part I

Again I return, wading knee depth,
Tide of tears flowing from the oppressed,
Frantic wailing accompanies flogging of sparks,
Enchanting mist of Grey now penetrating the dark,
An echo masked by shadow startles them,
Oh how brave they have all been,
I shudder and retreat,
In bare feet,
She looms over me,
Mistress of the bloody sea,
Helpless as she assists my drowning,
Corruption of her mind by Sir growling.

Part II

I shake my head.
I turn away.
I think instead.
I walk towards day.

Part III

My opinion on this land is governed by only one,
Not by a Sir, Master, Mistress, Dame or Dom,
My journey to sea is complete and now I know,
That my vessel of return can't be sunk by those,
My birdsong will rise and drown the red tide,
Fluttering wing of the eagle signals my pride.

Part IV

I have been here before,
Unwanted and left sore,
Spanked time and again,
Blood signaling the end.

Part V

The enemy shall never walk over me,
Nor bide with me in my safe den.

MRS SEXPERT

Mrs Sexpert was hurt, bound to wheels,
She still emitted that magical appeal,
Of that feeling of when you court,
Or of something you should not ought,
As now her injury had settled in,
Time had passed by from prior sin,
A vice had now turned to must,
Her mind focused on lust.

Canvassing across the land,
Summoning for a firm hand,
With a roll of French tongue,
She unbridled a man's son,
Via a request of poetic woo,
That would cast her own dew,
And warm her searing heart,
Despite their distance apart.

With trembling hands he admitted,
This must have been a special submit,
To service such a request,
From one inspiring love nest,
He blanked out his own mind,
To write words that are so kind,
Despite it a personal request,
He always aspired to his best.

With mind blanketed with thought,
Dreaming of things he should not,
Mixed images of beautiful maid,
His caring and deliver of aid,
If her deep eyes should flutter,
Would surely cast him to stutter,
But her request would never age,
So he cast words upon the page.

Trapped amidst time and space,
Averted gaze at angelic face,
Too far away for lips to touch,
Or taste her Venus as such,
Nor able to rest head on breast,
Could not swim into her crest,
Forced to stay calm while apart,
Yet able to hear a beating heart.

Tempted to the edge of mind,
By human spirit being so kind,
Still lured to impale with thrust,
And request to satisfy her must,
The poet would still apply,
Lyrics to harvest her small writhe,
Seeking thoughts that would urge,
Her hidden water to silently surge.

Words churn from what he should not,
To dark thoughts searing red hot,
Penetrating shallow cave of lust,
Enslaving him to heavy thrust,
Fingers entangled in his hair,
Quenching his thirst down there,
Arched and spread wide apart,
Finally she felt her own heart.

Rapidly rising with the beat,
Her hunger for flesh and meat,
Fingers compelled without delay,
To spill her hidden waters away,
The curse from her French tongue,
Now requesting they become one,
Invoking a cry from rapid pace,
With struggle beneath silk and lace.

The son of man now suspends,
In thought that should never end,
As all words that evolve over time,
Die out, except those that rhyme,
The poet submits what he imagined,
And close this journey of passion,
Content with a single sigh,
of her smile, flutter, and eye.

REBORN

Late one night under a moonlight glow,
I questioned my life and alter-ego,
Am I the dunderhead that had it all wrong?
Was I just a chorus in someone else's song?

Reminiscing to the voice of an owl,
Wondering what life really meant now,
Other than surviving my own death each night,
I am incapable of separating wrong from right.

Idling along the highway so grey,
I watched as the reaper took his life away,
Caught up in traffic without any flow,
The ambulance left with nowhere to go.

That day I'd worn a suit like a senator,
Living the dream to be a cash generator,
Climbing corporate walls to climb out of the gutter,
These elusive heights turning me into a nutter.

Foul stench of the land drifting upwind,
Falling from man and his infernal sin,
I continued to wipe the dried salt from my eye,
With memories fading of that time passing by.

With the crowd I abscond from the dream,
Into a reality that's virtually unseen,
Submitting myself to now live with the hoards,
I wrapped my torn wrists from where blood poured.

TRAIN

It's my stop,
Train pulls in,
She's riding up front,
I raise brow & grin.

"All Aboard" is the call,
I fit my cap,
Propped against wall,
Sat in my lap.

The heat from my boiler,
Singes her thigh,
Rapidly I recoil her,
Teardrop from eye.

Mister, will you,
Cup your mouth?
"Chew, Chew, Chew"
Down … err … "South."

Will you, my lover,
Wrap fingers into fist,
"Chugga, Chugga, Chugga"
It would be so bliss.

The pistons pumping,
Wheels spinning,
Heart is thumping,
Ecstatic grinning.

Her whistle blows,
"Whoo, Whoo, Whoooooo"
Flushed with hot glow,
Soaked through.

FRIEND

The sweeper was there in the club that day,
But I was busy and could not afford to stay,
He donated his time and gave us a smile,
The next day he dropped after running a mile.

The red-nosed gentleman always said hi,
Eager to hear how my day had gone by,
Regardless of what went on in his life,
I heard of his death by his gracious wife.

We drove down the road, cursed at the car,
Even with doctors attending right there,
Casually labeling the stranger a jerk,
The stranger remained, never made it to work.

My Grandfather always seemed grumpy & mean,
Until one afternoon he coughed up his spleen,
He was strong willed and always merry with beer,
My last words had made my feelings quite clear.

The dust barely settles as he falls on foreign soil,
A journalist captures the moment blood spoils,
Of uniformed father with his kids at home,
Who learn of his death when online they roam.

I sit in my bunker and peer through my eyes,
Hiding from this world and my untimely demise,
Calmly putting everything to the test,
Running from the night where I never rest.

My existence lives in a corridor of time,
Caring for lives who are not mine,
Rolling messages and pages of words,
Content with ending if I am ever heard.

BLOOM

I am besieged by his inner beauty and charm,
How could I resist his darkened presence?
He informed me he would employ no harm,
But to expect the deepest love, with his full intent.

In his own words,
To be fucked entirely until breathless.

That was days ago and now I wait,
He has barely cast anything but a cold eye,
Calculating when I shall become his ripened bait,
I pass through time in one long cruel sigh.

I cannot believe,
This epic love scene is owed to me.

A vibration sounds within my hand,
Travelling upward through to my heart,
No matter where you are in this land,
I will soon enter where you part.

I now knew,
His journey of lust was our next destiny.

The warmth swam around my mind,
He broke me down with glass of wine,
A perfect evening to unwind,
He was so gentle and very kind.

My body pulsed,
As my secret desires became unlocked.

By the fire we lay upon deep pile,
The melody trickled across my ears,
Last penetration had been such a while,
I was lost in his gaze with soul so sincere.

My mind swooned,
I now yearned to be sabotaged by him.

A request was made to adorn satin upon lace,
Entranced I could not ignore,
Upon return I was ambushed by his embrace,
Barely through the bedroom door.

His teeth tugged my lip,
The firm grasp flooded my inner core.

His words cascaded across my face,
One thousands kisses will not suffice,
Goddess stretched within her space,
Her hooded guise no longer spliced.

The cool air breeze,
Had now begun to enrapture me.

Torn apart from our embossed lips,
Unable to capture critical breath,
His attention turning to my hips,
And my sanctuary under lace leaves.

My fingers coiled,
Through his perfumed locks of hair.

Held fast from shoulder under my thigh,
Chanting invisibly into the still night,
And then echoes into a sudden cry,
As his tongue disappeared from sight.

He swam into me,
As my flooded plains broke away.

Amidst heady spell and mist of grey,
I finally caught my own breath,
As he raised to carry me away,
Towards white sheets upon still bed.

I pleaded for him,
To permeate his essence throughout me.

My flush peaked when firm grasp instead,
Captured my pulsating wrists,
Forcing them both above my head,
Before he spanked me on my bliss.

He growled hungrily,
His period of warning was now over.

Once again the mark was applied,
My body surged in sharp alarm,
Thrusting himself between my thighs,
Surging inside with lust's firearm.

I broke my hands free,
Ripping at his tight body to come even closer.

Settling into an earth shattering pace,
Foundations quaking with shaking lights,
We saturated each other in recoiled embrace,
Climatic devastation of any ounce of fight.

With his last motion,
He kissed my hooded bloom tenderly.

AMBROSIA

Sanctuary reigns amid warm luxurious cover,
Gold-banded flesh adorns captivated lover,
Boundless limits of lust sliced and carved within,
As if the gods of Erotes had drawn the incision.

Nymphs of fantasy taunt throughout the night,
Faded dreams embroil with erotic delight,
Seeking a moment that will forever last,
To shelter within cavern while the storm passes.

Wearily I wake from the depth of my lover's dream,
Cast into turbulent waters by a soul that's unseen,
Yet her eyes reach forth and signal so certain,
She seeks swollen depth to part her moist curtain.

I secure leather collar to my lust torn pet,
Burning intensely her fire of soft red velvet,
Moist lips touching to anoint desert that is parched,
My entwined fingers ensure her neck arches.

Her sensuality and flesh propels me to float,
Passionate wet kisses placed upon her soft throat,
I slice through her curtain and wet leading edge,
Come closer to within me becomes her spoken pledge.

The serpent slowly rises as a King to the throne,
Quivering with scent and sight of precious dome,
Amid rich treacle and gush of sweet innocence,
She beckons me to join her with vigorous relent.

Like a stone plunged into a deep still pond,
Ripples fan out from my scorching hot wand,
My firm hand delivers five slivers of pain,
Her sudden cry of ecstasy resounds like rain.

Her face soon adorns a flush of pink glow,
As my stream of white hot foam now flows,
Locked together we embrace each other's soul,
As the ambrosia of lust swirls within her bowl.

BREACHED

Slowly I gather my senses as my lust torn patience stands on trial,
This force is relentless crudely triggered by your smile.

My dampened spirit holds no remorse plotting your pleasurable pain,
The internal conflict edges me toward boundaries of sane.

Exhaustion dispels rose-colored cement of searing maiden,
My agile mind quivers upon exit of your haven.

Within that moment of silence we dance motionlessly within your crest,
Aromatic mist hovering like an angel's voice from your nest.

Shattered like glass you fall to rinse amber salts from the spill,
My cold sweat turning to vapor seeking a second fill.

With white stream rising I walk through the dripping wet cloth,
Sunlight embraces you as the river of essence drops.

My captivated gaze permeates to adorn your mirrored shadow,
Our lust flooded emotions drift within the shallows.

The thundering stream swirls with passion soft as spring rain,
Our search for lost love enchants me to a world of pain.

Beauty and grace enters me through tormented dark eye,
Aroused and swollen intent harnessed between your thighs.

Through entry of satin gate my rapid of pulsating blood rushes within,
My flesh is enraptured amidst the blissful sin.

Amidst cresting waves of surf flailing my skin under your nails,
Ambient noise of spring shower deafened by your hails.

You stood there before intent upon bathing within foaming lotion,
We now stand as heavenly bodies writhing with emotion.

Gently I part company before mighty plunge of imminent return,
Immersed and soaked within depth of lusts churn.

The mighty earth cracks open as we arrive together within a dream,
Destiny breached forever while our souls are lost within the steam.

EXIST

I'm waiting for one of those calls,
That involves a dear friend,
May not have seen him since last fall,
But E-N-D still spells end.

He is in good hands,
Or so they all say,
Tagged name in a band,
In case it's needed the next day.

Near departed souls of land,
Maybe someone else's mate,
Who may need a new patch,
Prior to knock on the gate.

Or possibly sent toward pitch,
Because life is a cruel bitch,
With broken beggars on the street,
At the rich man's feet.

So time stays dead still,
Words echo through my room,
Shaking from lack of pill,
Least there is no more rat boom.

We fill our soul while we sit,
Wash our salts and quench,
Food never fills this deep pit,
We all are players in the shit.

A bell signals message of news,
To earth our personal fears,
A few words would induce spew,
Others would bring cheers.

The mighty power of words,
Delivers more that deep shock,
Nervously, I write some blurbs,
My emotions kept in stock.

It is still a beautiful day,
Blue skies and clouds in sky,
It is what some people may say,
A fantastic day to die.

If there is ever such time,
Place or ideal situation,
Life's passage of rhyme,
Sends tingles of sensation.

Last night when she called,
There was panic in her voice,
Obviously she had balled,
As if there was one choice.

Hey, that's what they do,
The white coats and nurses,
"Here is the honest truth,
As you fill our purses",
We all help if we're able,
And say well be there,
As they're spread out on table.

That's our worse fear,
But I have done what I can,
For my friend torn in pieces,
He always knew who I am.

A man of few words,
I just sit still on this hill,
I know death will persist,
I write when my mind is still,
I bleed daily to exist.

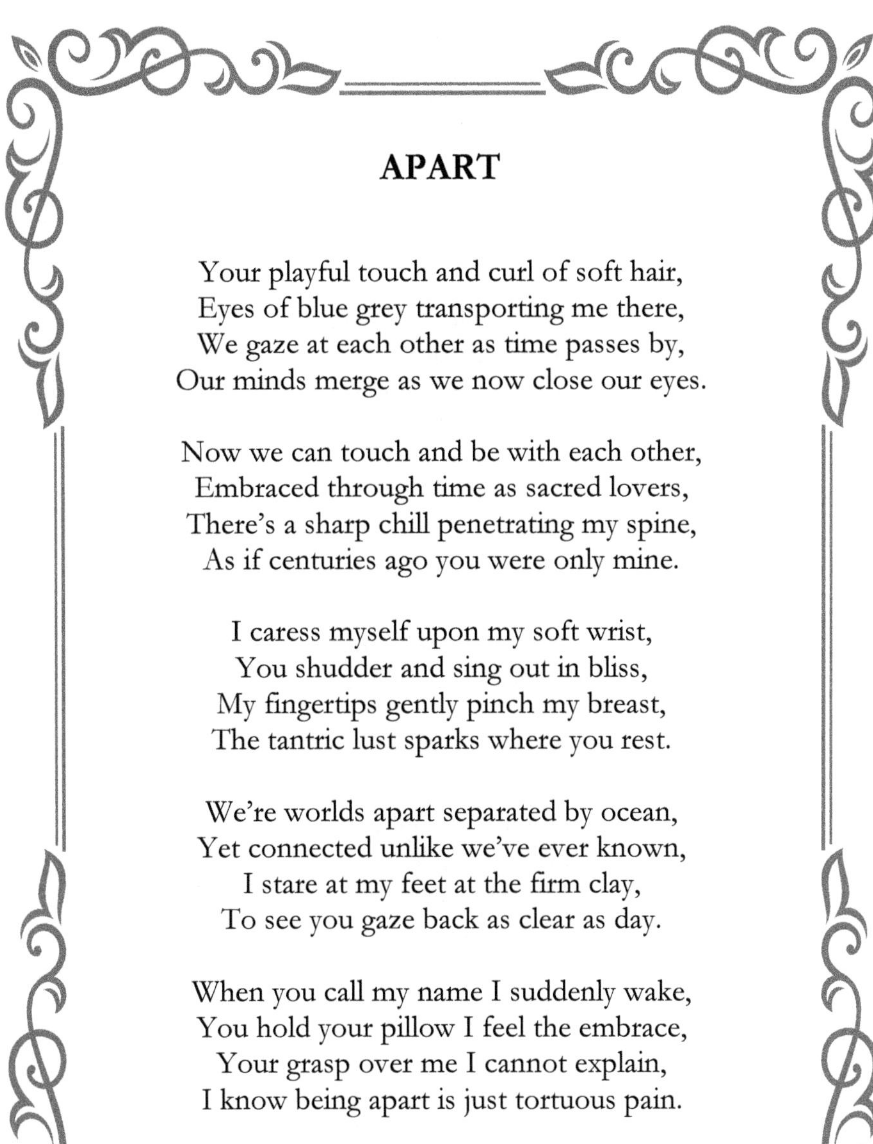

APART

Your playful touch and curl of soft hair,
Eyes of blue grey transporting me there,
We gaze at each other as time passes by,
Our minds merge as we now close our eyes.

Now we can touch and be with each other,
Embraced through time as sacred lovers,
There's a sharp chill penetrating my spine,
As if centuries ago you were only mine.

I caress myself upon my soft wrist,
You shudder and sing out in bliss,
My fingertips gently pinch my breast,
The tantric lust sparks where you rest.

We're worlds apart separated by ocean,
Yet connected unlike we've ever known,
I stare at my feet at the firm clay,
To see you gaze back as clear as day.

When you call my name I suddenly wake,
You hold your pillow I feel the embrace,
Your grasp over me I cannot explain,
I know being apart is just tortuous pain.

THE GLOBAL NIGHTMARE

I'm restless tonight,
All we do is fight,
Across mother earth,
Blood puddles in her dirt.

The soldiers we see,
Under uniform bleed,
Gunshots silent any voice,
Freedom is their choice.

Our children stand bare,
Next to volunteers,
Still many will fall,
Cannot save them all.

Red and blue light spin,
Running fugitive grins,
Observers simply look,
As the innocent are hooked.

Headline man leaves wife,
Amidst global strife,
To provide her a grin,
He mistook as a sin.

We wish to discover,
A new inner lover,
Who never denies,
Our fullest desires.

It's human nature you see,
To tear fruit from the tree,
To love one another,
Yet kill someone's brother.

When is it enough?
To discover true love,
Amidst our war tears,
Beneath our real fears.

Turn my reality away,
With fantasy foreplay,
I lay awake when,
This dream never ends.

STING

The sting was applied bare,
Handed as Sir stood there,
To my pulsating grace,
Through his steady embrace.

Quivering head to toe,
I wished he'd impale me so,
But that was never my choice,
Listening to his command of voice.

Once, then two times more,
He spanked until I was sore,
Carefully checking with each burst,
Asking if & how I was hurt.

Such compassion from this man,
I was born to live by his hand,
As he gently parted my lips,
With his red-hot fingertips.

Heat from his palm glowed,
As he delivered to me so,
Tenderly above my thigh,
To weep but never a cry.

Gently he would now soothe,
Attentive in every move,
Gently rolling over my bust,
Building my edge full of lust.

Without uttering any word,
His entry made me squirm,
Sensing his passage inside,
To my surging moist reside.

My heart stared to melt,
As his girth began to swell,
Beneath my moist Venus,
Demise of light between us.

His domain ventured deep,
As I now began to seep,
His touch is like none other,
Guiding my first shudder.

Despite being red and sore,
He asked if I wished for more,
Query then turned to demand,
As my waves met his command.

Soaked through with my musk,
I savored his passionate tusk,
He penetrated me with his girth,
Delivering his sacred surge.

As if struck by mighty clout,
I clenched to his ivory spout,
As he gently rocked my earth,
Satisfying me beyond my worth.

Cradled in my lover's embrace,
Entombed with statuesque grace,
Softly whispering into my ear,
I love you with pain, my dear.

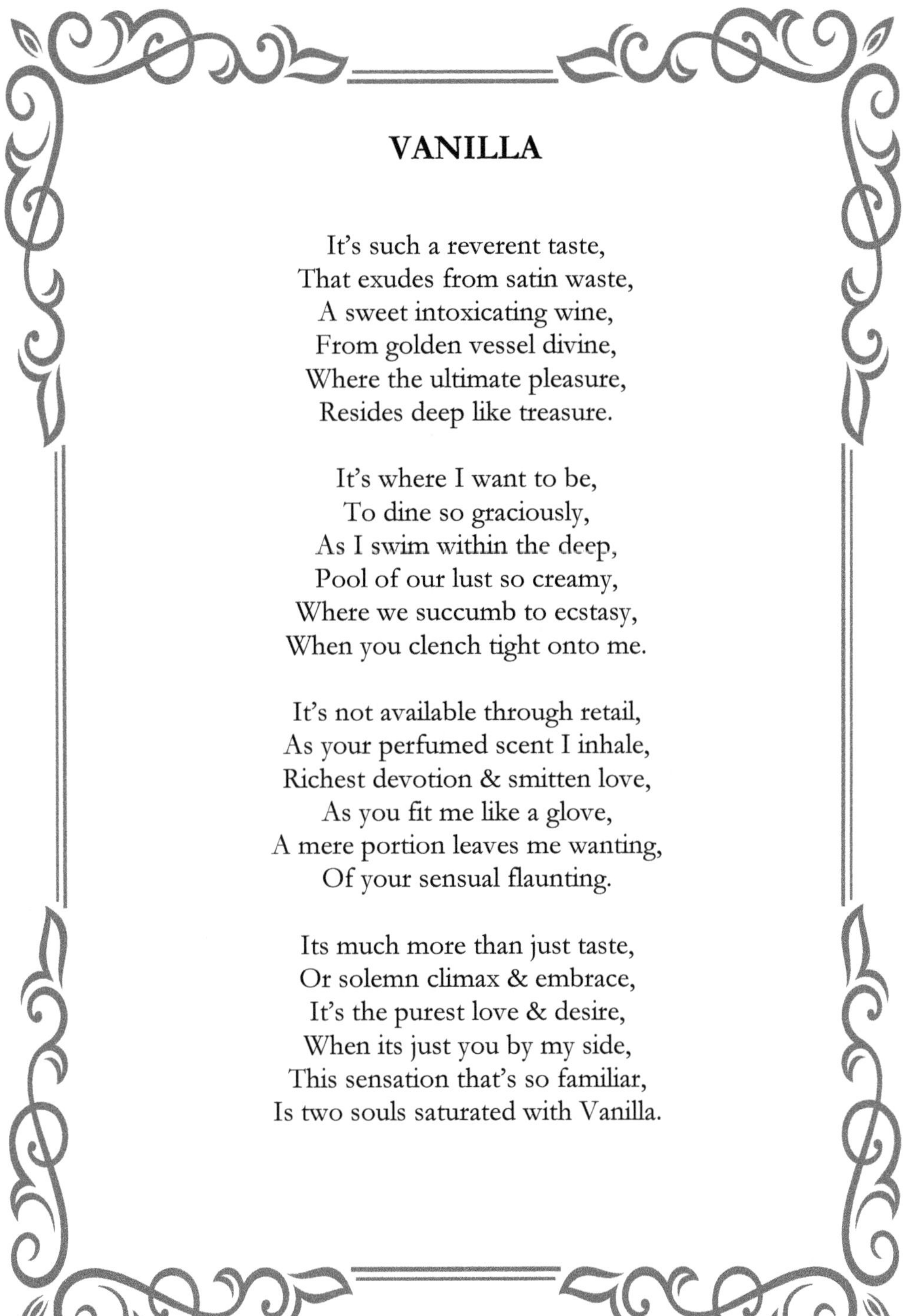

VANILLA

It's such a reverent taste,
That exudes from satin waste,
A sweet intoxicating wine,
From golden vessel divine,
Where the ultimate pleasure,
Resides deep like treasure.

It's where I want to be,
To dine so graciously,
As I swim within the deep,
Pool of our lust so creamy,
Where we succumb to ecstasy,
When you clench tight onto me.

It's not available through retail,
As your perfumed scent I inhale,
Richest devotion & smitten love,
As you fit me like a glove,
A mere portion leaves me wanting,
Of your sensual flaunting.

Its much more than just taste,
Or solemn climax & embrace,
It's the purest love & desire,
When its just you by my side,
This sensation that's so familiar,
Is two souls saturated with Vanilla.

ADIEU

She penetrated my life like a ray of light,
Tumbling around my feet,
Like the painfully loved girl she yearned to be.

The deepest curiosity had her wanting in need,
She hoped I could help,
Drenched she then clambered from the rocks.

My beacon of hope was in torment upon the sea,
Grey with absent souls,
I held her close with the others inside me.

The innocent child kept questioning and adoring,
Looking for answers,
We grew fonder and loved each other as true friends.

When the walls collapsed around she returned a favor,
She held me close to her heart,
I thought to myself nothing could tear us apart.

Before I knew the innocent child had grown wings,
Along with other angels,
My sanctuary faded as dust settled with their absence.

I watched them as their Master like a father would his children,
They flourished like flowers,
My Mon Amie were departing to sail seas of their own.

We had all laughed, cried, cared, shared, and bared,
We have loved one another,
Shattered soul being held together by their glue.

When my angel of destiny appeared before me,
I knew the end would appear,
Inside I always knew and feared it would happen.

The day Alice died I was caught staggering and empty handed,
Her ship appeared lost,
The sea I plucked her from had taken her soul away from us.

She then appeared before me like a shadow cast in a dream,
Rescued by her own master,
I smiled then as I do now knowing she was in safe hands.

I never collared her as a pet or touched her as a slave,
Simply cared for her as true friend,
My deepest sincerity had now turned to tragic epiphany.

Tears now tumble down my face as if the sea of pain,
Had burst inside of me,
Pouring from my chin I can not help myself but grin.

Shattered through I feel torn to shreds by the few,
Who really stood by at the time,
And for whom I have devoted my soul to in black and white.

This pain searing through me is nothing more than a goodbye,
More likely see you soon,
It hurts so much worse, yet so much better, due to our compassion.

I know their departure and absence is never for too long,
While we answer each other's call,
Yet these tears of fantasy drench me in my reality.

A reality within which,
My only wish,
We will never say Adieu.

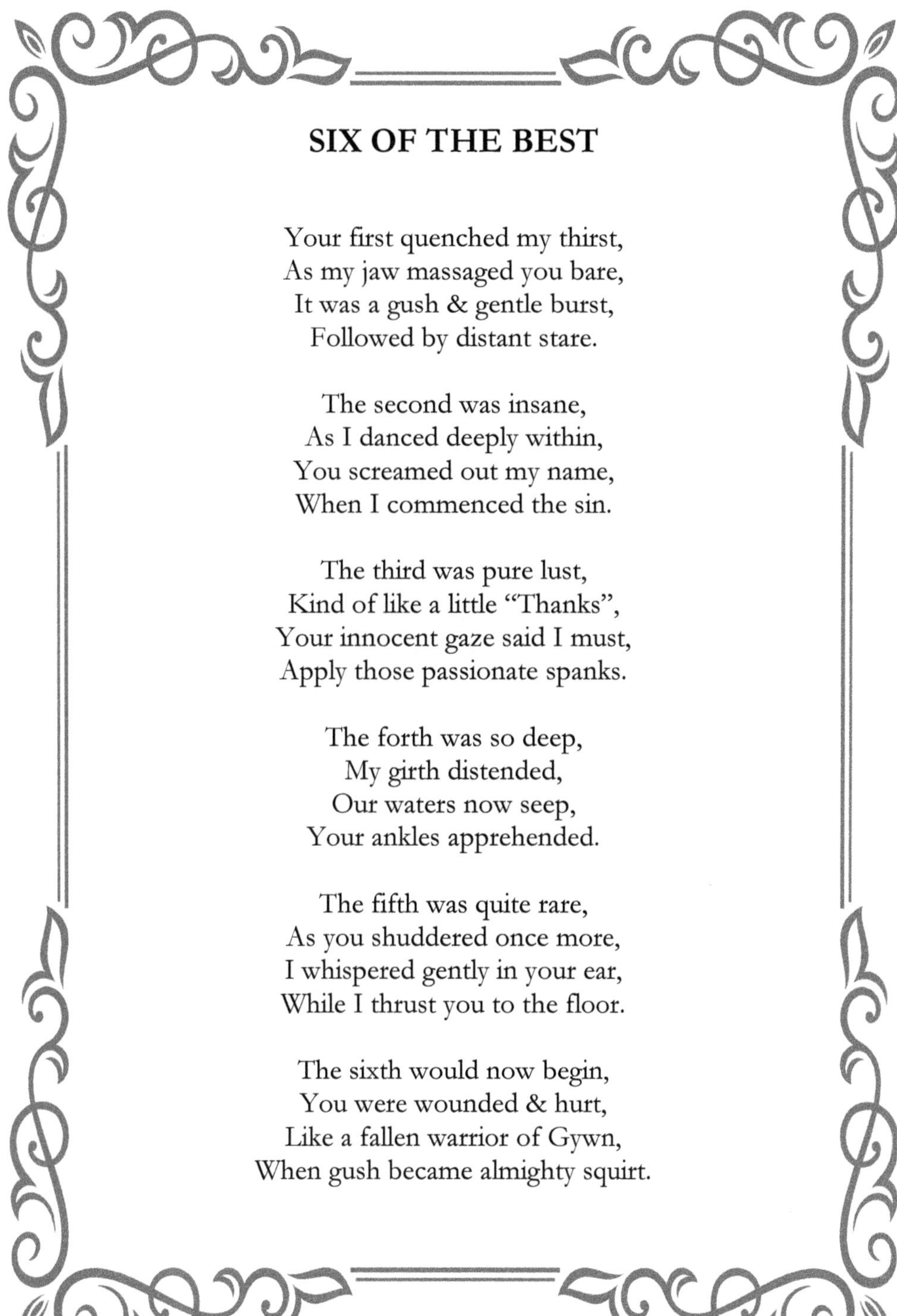

SIX OF THE BEST

Your first quenched my thirst,
As my jaw massaged you bare,
It was a gush & gentle burst,
Followed by distant stare.

The second was insane,
As I danced deeply within,
You screamed out my name,
When I commenced the sin.

The third was pure lust,
Kind of like a little "Thanks",
Your innocent gaze said I must,
Apply those passionate spanks.

The forth was so deep,
My girth distended,
Our waters now seep,
Your ankles apprehended.

The fifth was quite rare,
As you shuddered once more,
I whispered gently in your ear,
While I thrust you to the floor.

The sixth would now begin,
You were wounded & hurt,
Like a fallen warrior of Gywn,
When gush became almighty squirt.

I MISSED YOU

I missed you last night,
And the night before,
So many voices in my life,
With latches upon my door.

Should we meet once again,
With suggestive voice so kind,
I would consider you my friend,
To swim deep within my mind,
And to rise on distant shore,
Where the sun always shines,
You observe, I prepare to pour,
Lust rinses the sands of time.

Glazed look through glowing glass,
We fulfill each other's empty soul,
Though this moment rarely lasts,
My savage beast remains in control.

Through the words that I write,
We survive from day to day,
Fantasy of distant flight,
When I sing, "sway baby sway",
During my tearful Lovers Lullaby.

Embracing passion within our pain,
As I sleep within the night,
While you walk amidst the rain,
Although neither crosses the bight,
Though a Gentleman never should,
We spill out oceans every time,
Treading carefully within the wood.

'Til the warm light returns to me,
And darkness turns you blind,
Our pain remains separated by the seas,
Our passion captured in common time.

DARE

I wish you were there,
To wipe away tears,
Drawn from my fear,
Washing me bare.

As my heart sears,
I am not prepared,
Been many years,
I have no more flair.

My trade has become stare,
Eroded soul was sincere,
Now it has been sheared,
Ripped beyond repair.

Lust destroyed our care,
Passion cannot compare,
You think I'm queer,
Maybe having affair.

Not answering cheers,
Your silk touch rare,
Long nights have disappeared,
Your kiss is insincere.

I'm pushed to despair,
Fury inside flares,
My unanswered prayer,
My soul is where?
Within poetic lair.

To tear fruit from the tree,
To love one another,
Yet kill someone's brother.
When is it enough?

Now it rains tears,
Violent winds ensnare,
Love is not a dare,
I was always there.

THRILL GIRL

When I was young before I fathered a son,
I met a cute girl who was always up for the thrill,
With her long blonde hair and pleated tartan mini skirt,
She really loved close affection and playing with dirt.

Way back then she was one of my closest friends,
How she loved to pretend and make herself glisten,
With complete abandonment and without a care,
We would play with dolls and teddies during BJ & The Bear.

Motionless I would lay for her as she used me to play,
In the shed out back galvanized with holes of light,
She abused me and touched me to her own delight.

I was only a boy.
I was barely a toy.

Yet she played with me there without any real care,
To her own sexual delight while I vowed not to fight,
I was only there at her leisure for her own selfish pleasure.

When finished with me she sighed said goodbye and went inside,
Leaving me to pull them up and walk alone with my pup,
She would shout abuse at me when I looked away from her,
As she showed me buttons and ripples under the skirt,
Telling how much to put on and when to stop pressing in.

I was nearly a teen.
I was hideously obscene.

She knew the time was right when I would become ripe,
I was her toy and secret friend that she wanted to the end,
But she liked to share and did so when her friends were there,
Taking turns with my flesh and washing over me with mess,
Telling me not to fight or they tell my keepers they might,
Keeping me as secret as any fuck toy could ever be,
Slowly filling the dam that will burst through insanity.

I was never a man.
I would cry when I can.

BE SINCERE

From the moment I saw you,
My hunger for lust began,
I knew that I needed you,
To make me what I am.

To love and caress you,
And play with each other,
Capturing your honey dew,
As would any great lover.

Your flame almost vanquished,
But heart locked down,
Your desire drawn in anguish,
Despite living in foreign town.

Magnitudes by your beauty,
Talent and grace,
Life fell all around me,
Heart quickened in pace.

I stared at the walls,
Pressing onto my head,
Thoughts started to crawl,
About us together in bed.

I was now entrapped,
Lost in your charms,
Desired and unwrapped,
Melting in your arms.

My pillar of fear rising,
Upon a distant star,
Falling to heaven,
Landing where you are.

An angel armed,
With heart shaped arrow,
I was alert and alarmed,
A romance I could not borrow.

My heart had been snapped,
Many times before,
By girls like yourself,
Who have cast me to floor.

Should I be distant,
Or fearful in your sight,
Consider the instant,
My passion went and took flight.

When you entered my life,
Upon distant land,
Walking from strife,
To me love unplanned.

My heart is caught,
Between harbor and shore,
I want to take flight,
To meet you and more.

RESTRAINT – PJ BAYLISS

MISTRESS Z'S INVITE

Too exhausted to wake,
I slyly dope myself up,
Upon a blue that was cut,
Before contaminating my gut.

I'm covered in funk,
Not excrement from junk,
This funk is so kind,
Oozing from my mind.

I turn my attention to,
One of a few,
My promised visit,
To one so exquisite.

I lay down the line:
Mon Ami had called,
With a scene that enthralled,
To preclude Mick's Reward,
Her heartbeat soared.

I set path to visit,
Lover's remit,
Suggesting to she,
To be Mistress to me.

She liked the idea of which,
Suggested I switch.

MISTRESS Z'S INTRODUCTION

Cabbie roused me from my dream,
"Yo fella we're here it seems",
I opened an eye,
Said "it'll be fine".

No matter where I was,
I scoffed; there'll be a good time,
It's my dream,
Those are my rules.

Its apocalyptic flash,
Details overlooked,
Knocked on door,
Chains rattled,
She looked,
"Who are you?",
Silently I showed,
Tattoo on my wrist.

Her face glowed,
"Mon Ami", she gasped,
Releasing the hatch,
Letting me past.

"Let the game begin",
I announced with a grin,
You ordered a switch,
Hope you don't pounce.

Her priceless look,
Wet tears across her lip,
Dormant breath from open jaw,
My alerts were checked.

Not the first time I'd been tabled,
"Where shall I start?"
She queried when able,
I thrust my black locker bag,
Upward from floor.

"Well Mistress Z,
You're gonna treat me like a whore,
Spiked heels are a must,
Roller wheels that cut,
Some bondage tape,
Cuckold devices for role play rape."

"A gimp if required,
Mask if so desired,
Anything you ever wished,
Use my bag of tricks."

Hungrily she spotted my gear,
Not knowing when to start or where,
I silently shut the door,
Let's work it out some more.

My Blue kicking in,
Take some time to plan,
And tell this story when we can.

I'm not beginning at the end,
I'll reveal when I wake up my friend,
'Til tomorrow…. Misery with Mistress Z

MISERY WITH MISTRESS Z

I contemplated my fate awaiting me that night,
Careful preparation of the long haul flight,
With black leather zip bag and tools within,
To strip me barren and potentially remove skin,
Her game of choice was to take out her anger,
Frustration and nightmares upon a mere stranger,
As none were willing, physically able or devout,
I conceded to her whim due to her undeniable pout.

Exit of flight and modern chariot to her door,
I knocked only once when footsteps crossed floor,
Click of lock, the chain rattled before door creak,
She looked at me twice and asked if I was the freak,
So I rolled up my sleeve to reveal wrist tattoo,
Assured she cried "Mon Ami that is really you?"
With black bag and leather shoes I entered,
Prepared for hours ahead of lust and torment.

Our arrangement was simply to switch Sub with Dom,
She wore the boots, rubber gloves and used tongs,
With the notion being for me to eat what I feed,
And suffer misery 'til the edge of me bleeds,
With the embracing caress of Z's bottom lip,
She dispatched me into place with her leather whip,
Immediately casting me to the floor to her knee,
Her next command was to lick her boots tenderly.

Her emotions surging from cold dam of real life,
She just wanted to release them by emitting strife,
Upon sight of my lips caressing her heeled toe,
Mistress erupted with full force to inflict woe,
"Pet will now rise" hauling me to my feet,
As the bag was searched for my leather leash,
"Pet shall not cry, no matter what comes as pain,
Or upon the cross you shall be burnt through my fane."

My leash had a twitch barely three inches wide,
Used to secure and restrain my male pride,
From there the chain stretched up to my neck,
With a couple of twists, I became cherry red,
No cuff between ankles but chained between toes,
Wearing leather mask with pinholes for my nose,
My final restraint does not fit many folk,
Is a solid wooden beam: The Withers Yolk.

Mistress inspected my costume with stance,
Circling me slowly within a sensual dance,
"Pet looks appealing" she spoke to me at last,
My murmur of accord cut off so fast,
Her delicate palm slapped across my face,
Followed by her lips and tender embrace,
Her force of lust pumped me full of energy,
"When I'm through Pet you'll come inside me."

Her message increased flow of blood to my pride,
Being hard as steel was generally her guide,
The sight of my member bringing her to pink,
But that only made her realize and think,
Of her lover who ignored her so many times,
Now she craved every inch of what was once mine,
Her lips sealed my glans before gathering speed,
And eased off before I considered blurt of my seed.

"Don't even think about it Pet" sang my Mistress,
She paddled my nates while caressing my midriff,
To punish me sanctimoniously for being a mumbler,
She forced me down to all fours with steel humbler,
Her words "Be still now Pet" melted me right there,
A double-ended phallus sewed us together as a pair,
She eased it deep into me as I groaned in pleasure,
Steadily riding me at her own pace in her leisure.

Mistress inched and then shoved as I ballooned with blood,
She edged herself to the limit of her goddess's flood,
Sensing my own precious moment, her crop unleashed,
Across my firm shoulders taming my imminent release,
Not a word I could utter as she continued to butter,
My inners climbed upward to climatic stutter,
Silently she cursed before sliding herself off,
To unzip my mask and forcing me to quaff.

My thirst felt like dust as I gorged her musk,
Follicles of hair were yanked as she thrust,
Gasping for air my instincts soon kicked in,
As I unleashed my tongue to swim in her sin,
Her spiked heels picked up and dug into my thighs,
I was racked with tension as tears filled my eyes,
Her heart-broken moan flooded my cheeks,
Yet I was still dry and left thirsty to peak.

She released my mask without a moment to spare,
Rolled onto my back as Mistress stood and glared,
Then she whispered "Pet this is going to hurt",
She clamped my nipple with a chain to where I blurt,
Pain intensified if I dared to move forward or back,
As my precious Mistress had given me no slack,
Then she slowly trampled my chest with her heels,
I spared not one muscle as my senses reeled.

Broken and shattered, scarred lovingly in red,
Mistress grasped my leash and led me to bed,
Four pillared post where the rope intertwined,
Spoken softly, "Pet will only be nourished by mine"
She anchored my limbs; the rope did not pinch,
I was firmly distended 'till I could not move an inch,
Then my head jerked up and eyes fixed upon the rafter,
Her moist tongue lapped and rolled around my shaft.

The sensual brink of my own outburst was so near,
I was determined not to show my Mistress any fear,
The clamps hammered down while blood filled me tight,
"Pet will not come" I must avoid with every might,
The chain broke loose and my flesh nearly tore,
As she now eased me inside her delicate bore,
Her majestic body began hovering slowly over me,
Every motion edging me closer to release my seed.

Every writhe and thrust was forced with intention,
All the time I was told never to mention,
Any safe-word or verse as I needed to trust,
That our perfect moment would come when it must,
She was deeply impaled on me at every incline,
Vigorously she rocked upon my rooted vine,
Her back arched back and all hell broke loose,
As her dam burst open down my thighs like a sluice.

Saturated and soaked from Mistress's burst of lust,
I felt shipwrecked and shredded as she raised her husk,
My throbbing red fare left steaming from her banquet,
Breathless she whispered, "You have pleased me my Pet,
For this you shall now be rewarded for lasting so long,
I command you to take me from behind with your schlong"
There was no delay in servicing my Mistress's plea,
As I slowly inserted myself as she knelt upon knee.

Desolated I implanted my rigid flesh deeply within,
Mistress Z's delicate, moist, and voluptuous rim,
Easing forward until darkness shrouded my glans,
I grasped her red corset with my trembling hands,
"You will remain still Pet as I must take control"
I braced myself rigid and tight so as not to roll,
"You will not come either" was her next command,
I truly was her fuck-toy satisfying every demand.

Patiently withstanding Mistress Z's ebb and flow,
Under her strict command not to come or go,
Bodies bathed in sweet lotion from her recent rain,
Gluteus and thigh muscles aching with sweet pain,
No other woman had I caressed so lovingly inside,
Gently fusing within her silk purse where I reside,
Her luxurious passage slowly grinding my love shaft,
When she picked up the pace I knew it wouldn't last.

Vigorously pumping me with everything she had,
Ramming my final inch inside her upon our love pad,
"Don't let me down Pet, take me all the way there"
My pulsating girth ensuring no room was spare,
Casually my hand drifted towards her pleasure zone,
Upon touch Mistress Z emitted a passionate moan,
Trembling and quaking while inner goddess climaxed,
Clenching to me tight until her glorious body relaxed.

Intoxicated with her scent as it burnt the still air,
The battered fuck-toy resonated with silent despair,
Splattered with moist lust, aching in deep pain,
Mistress Z slithered from upon top my love vein,
Tenderly touching the steel helmet of my member,
Pressure applied to goddess's steaming hot ember,
"Come for me Pet." her voice came to me as delight,
Rich essence gushed reverently upon her wings of flight.

My feet firmly planted while I touched sacred ground,
Our bodies gathered together as neither made a sound,
Her gentle smile returned before a gratifying sigh,
The burning fire disappeared from her gentle eye,
Touched upon chin, Mistress dispatched her last kiss,
Smiling she said "Pet you've delivered me such bliss."
My role as switch now expired, admiring her grace,
"I truly love you Peyton"… "I love you too, Chaise."

That gentle burning fire, now been purged from her eye,
Scented bodies of desire, spillage flowing down her thigh,
My chiseled body bare, she softly touched my rear end,
Grasp of what goes there, a tug released the dildo's end,
Blood surged with instant pitch; my cheeks relapse at last,
"I'm such a sorry bitch my Pet, for you're going to blast."
Flame returning to her eye, goddess rising within her snatch,
With submission, I sigh, committing to my next batch.

A yank of my chain, causing my emotions to be lost,
"I need a firm vein, you shall now adorn my cross",
Wrists bound above head, ankles bolted to the floor,
My clamp tightened until red, passionate lust from whore,
Then a whirr of power, tingling device runs over me,
Bound to her tower, I felt like a dam to the wild sea,
Buzzing my inner thigh, now my quivering perineum,
Tip of my erect desire, sending me into sweet delirium.

Clamped in steel vice, forcing me to remain harder still,
Frozen spike of ice, inserted into shaft of my quill,
The cold felt odd, yet prepped me for her next twist,
A long metal rod, placed inside felt painfully bliss,
Lubricated within, Mistress then clamped glistening rod,
To my swollen sin, with electrical pulse "Oh My God!"
Her charger ticked, as the blue pulse through me,
Igniting my thick, throbbing love shaft of ecstasy.

Cloaked in my mess, I bite lip, allowing pain to pass,
Mistress now dressed with a strap-on for my arse,
Release of my hands, now strapped to a large table,
Although bolted to stand, bent forward as far I'm able,
"Do you love Mistress?" she asks before the first punt,
I grunt in distress, "Wrong fucking answer you little runt!"
Tethered and bent, her glorious punishment impaled,
"Mistress I repent!"- Too late. One burst from her flail.

Threshold at test, flashbacks to my dark days gone by,
Scented love zest, I inhale pain by closing my eyes,
Mistress then clamps, the metal rod charges once again,
Silent pinging amps, scintillating sparks of cursed pain,
Flail swipes my flesh, my nirvana gradually descends,
Soothed by her thresh, orgasmic waves now blend,
"I am your lover…" Mistress's chorus rang in my ears,
Releasing my twitch, throbbing pleasure brings me to tears.

A quickening pace, her unbridled passion converging,
My retorted face, an eruptive climax emerging,
My musket fills, propelling metal rod like a canon,
Creamy seed spills, salvation gushes without abandon,
Amidst my desire, waves of energy emerge within,
Insatiable fire, as Aphrodite's lava pours from my sin,
Subdued, I relapse, plummeting with her divine grace,
Drifting I relax, waltzing with pleasure through subspace.

HARD WIRED

There was a girl,
Who loved the thrill,
Blonde hair, short skirt,
Loved playing with dirt.

She was once my friend,
Loved to pretend,
Without a care,
BJ & The Bear.

Motionless I would lay,
As she used me to play,
Shed with holes of light,
To her own delight.

I was only a boy,
Barely a toy,
Yet she played me there,
Without any care.

To her own delight,
I vowed not to fight,
I was there at her leisure,
For her own pleasure.

When I was finished,
She only sighed,
That is why
I'm hard wired.

ONCE BEFORE

I have been here once before,
Semiconscious,
Absent and fucked over,
Lying upon wooden floor,
In a desert of pain,
Upset,
Lonely and desperate,
At the end of Mother's chain.

I have died here once before,
Drowned,
Full of sea water,
Anchored to sea floor,
Rescued by his love,
Naked,
Tired and bedraggled,
Under shadow of white dove.

I have laughed here once before,
Tearfully,
Insane and happily,
Rolling all over the floor,
Cut open by my grin,
Paralyzed,
Split like a carcass,
Impervious to my own sin.

I have loved here once before,
Unconditionally,
Her admiration lasted,
Until buried under the floor,
Tortured and hurt,
Quietly,
By unknown offender,
Sick and twisted pervert.

I have flown here once before,
Endlessly,
Kept in business class,
World soaring under the floor,
Chasing that dream,
Endlessly,
Donating my weekends,
For nothing it now seems.

I have lived here once before,
Entombed,
Remains now rotten,
Once walking upon the floor,
My soul has been found,
Finally,
By destiny's angel,
Within the jaws of lusts hound.

I have been here once before,
Tormented,
By your love,
A shadow cast upon the floor,
Empty as a husk,
Barren,
Plastered into the wall,
Bathed within the light of dusk.

DEPARTING

Leave me alone, cant you see,
I'm trying to die here peacefully,
I can't understand why you hate,
The verse and words that I emulate.

The truth lies within obviously,
I am a lover and hater; creature from the sea,
I cry in the shower to disguise my tears,
My face doesn't alter to show my fears.

At night I would listen to them until I sleep,
Hoping for the day you will return to me,
I'm not in this life for the game anymore,
I'm bleeding inside where my heart was torn.

This is me inside flooding to bleed out,
To show the world what ME is all about,
I fight back the mist every single day,
You think I'm all here and with you to stay.

Smile is all I will ever take to my grave,
Not prepared to die so I shall misbehave,
I am completely lost at times within the trees,
I hope the path I follow will bring myself back to me.

RAPTURE

Don't deny me my true fate or destiny,
Promise you will corrupt every part of me,
Pledge your soul to accept me as one,
Vow not to spill any portion as I come.

Unleash your passion with your full force,
Never let anger determine our course,
Ensure I'm your one & only decadent sin,
Take me the whole distance within.

Never hold back any portion of trust,
Consume and devour every thrust,
Secure your kindred spirit with me,
Love and in return I'll set you free.

Tremble with delight as I implode,
Pouring within until you erode,
Climb with me to climatic stature,
Drink me in, as I am your rapture.

BURDEN

They say it is deep red,
Pumping rich blood to head,
Inane beating resounds inside,
Sharp pain flogging the mind.

Life's true essence exists,
Within black space akin to fist,
Rose petals cover my heart,
So easily ripped, torn apart.

Though dollar bills may fix the tear,
That blew apart when you were near,
Blood of my soul spilt for miles,
Coldly dripping from your smile.

Not interested in any repair,
Mere looks aggravate my fear,
Upon sight of my cheerful laughter,
They interrogate what I am after.

I only asked for one return,
To a question that now burns,
You silence my curious mind,
You make denial seem so kind.

Exhausted is your first excuse,
Now too late its just abuse,
Headache is yet another,
Illness becomes my early departure.

I could lay pitched here at night,
Waiting for your mighty flight,
Instead tears dampen my skin,
Rotting away my love within.

My salty ponds grow in doubt,
Tears ignite with flame from my pout,
Shattered heartbeat makes me tremble,
Emptying me of my former resemble.

I schedule life into me,
I see blood flow from me,
Leeched out from you no less,
Your innocence is my fucking mess.

What the bloody hell am I to do,
To turn back years not just these few,
You barely let me put a word in,
Packed tight I cram in more burden.

SENSUALITY

Insert a little piece of me,
Setting all inhibitions of lust free,
Unfold your soft wings while I tease,
Languishing within your unbridled seas.

Incarcerate me as I gently ease,
Stroking as I swim through seams,
Grasping me firm between your knees,
Unlocking your flooded heart with my key.

Sparks of desire ignite lust sprees,
Writhing with me amidst your pleas,
With golden engorged clasp you seize,
Your dam of devotion thawing from freeze.

Every ounce of your body agrees,
From passionate mind to swollen pea,
Explosive floodgate bursts in lost heave,
Amorous wave of fire beckons me not to leave.

Breathless you can only wheeze,
For I plunge steadily as we weave,
Scorching heat of intense flesh cleave,
Sobering abandonment you can't believe.

Linger a little longer please,
Rocking slowly amidst the breeze,
Hold me close in your arms & squeeze,
Consummate a little piece of my sensuality.

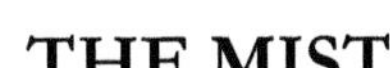

THE MIST

You do not see it,
Taste, or touch it,
It is simply there,
Like a blank stare,
A void it consumes,
Nothing else resumes,
It permeates and erodes you,
It commands and owns you,
It heeds no other master,
It serves no other.

My Mist
Feels Bliss.

PEN

A distant snap in the dark,
Creative spark,
I need the room… be gone please,
I need my own space,
To create,
Edit,
And compose.

Torment builds as I turn to look,
But she is already gone,
I panic inside,
& begin to cry.

Control,
My strings into my tormented soul,
Who the hell released this from my heart's hole?
The fog builds up,
My gas mask is applied,
The straps tighten up,
I'm knotted inside.

Passion builds,
It cannot be withheld,
Lust looms to the surface,
My body begins to swell.

Oh what has my newfound pride done?
I must remain calm.

Reaching below.
Release!
I must express!
I reach for my golden shaft,
So familiar to heart,
From the time I first unleashed it from the velvet purse,
And I write… sweet prose.
Sigh.

The distant snap echoes,
But deafens me in one strike.
The warmth and release of passionate tears.
I have found my deepest love,
One of writing to my fellow lovers and believers,
to help my warm heart build a path.

Now I am strong.
I know what I did wrong.
No one has the right to knock a king off his throne, so I decide.

Space, plan, time,
Strong heart,
And strong mind.

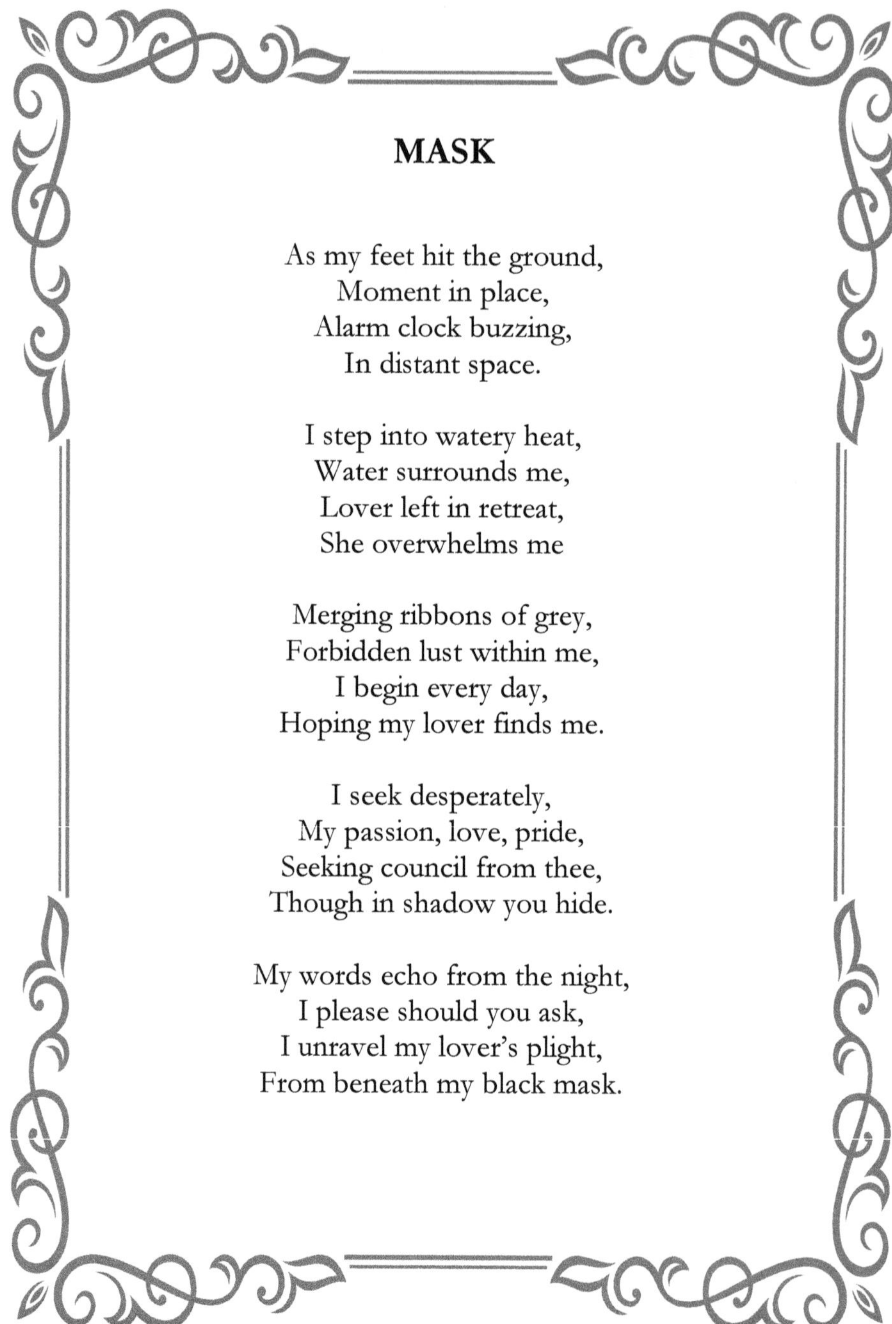

MASK

As my feet hit the ground,
Moment in place,
Alarm clock buzzing,
In distant space.

I step into watery heat,
Water surrounds me,
Lover left in retreat,
She overwhelms me

Merging ribbons of grey,
Forbidden lust within me,
I begin every day,
Hoping my lover finds me.

I seek desperately,
My passion, love, pride,
Seeking council from thee,
Though in shadow you hide.

My words echo from the night,
I please should you ask,
I unravel my lover's plight,
From beneath my black mask.

DUSK

A melancholy tear crosses his eye,
Yet another day passes by.

His idealistic thoughts are barred,
Raw emotions cut deep scars.

Bountiful passion lies within,
For whom he trusts and welcomes in.

Drained of lust until empty husk,
Replenished by the embers of dusk.

FORGOTTEN

I think of her with every breath,
She is as replenishing as life itself,
Her vapor resides upon the breeze,
Her essence within my mouth.

As I plunder within her watery depth,
Temperature rising,
Her beautiful eyes penetrate me,
Tingling writhing.

With firm grip she embraces me,
Intent to never part,
Naive girl does not realize,
Her tight hold of my heart,
The darkness tightens around her eyes.

I bind the knot,
My shadow cast upon silken thigh,
All sense of time forgotten.

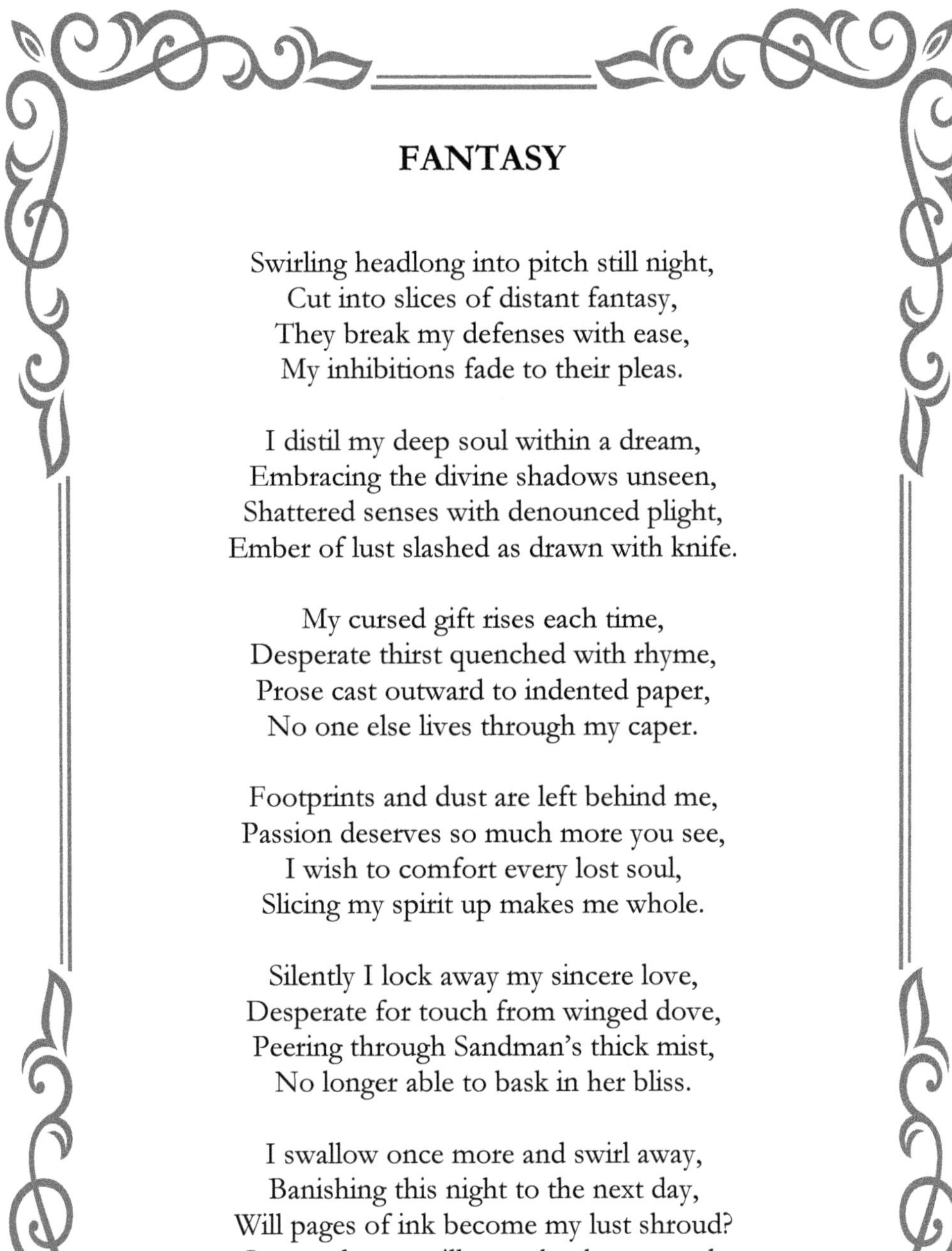

FANTASY

Swirling headlong into pitch still night,
Cut into slices of distant fantasy,
They break my defenses with ease,
My inhibitions fade to their pleas.

I distil my deep soul within a dream,
Embracing the divine shadows unseen,
Shattered senses with denounced plight,
Ember of lust slashed as drawn with knife.

My cursed gift rises each time,
Desperate thirst quenched with rhyme,
Prose cast outward to indented paper,
No one else lives through my caper.

Footprints and dust are left behind me,
Passion deserves so much more you see,
I wish to comfort every lost soul,
Slicing my spirit up makes me whole.

Silently I lock away my sincere love,
Desperate for touch from winged dove,
Peering through Sandman's thick mist,
No longer able to bask in her bliss.

I swallow once more and swirl away,
Banishing this night to the next day,
Will pages of ink become my lust shroud?
I press deeper still to make them proud.

NINETY MINUTES

It was about three,
She lay there, restless,
Sprawled up against me,
I became restless.

Like a lump of cloth linen,
Freshly washed in a pile,
I longed to be within,
I felt the need to defile.

In perfect state she lay,
Quietly pulsating,
And I knew that she may,
Want to feel the thrill. Zing.

In slumber I cupped,
Her with one hand,
And the other I rested,
Upon sacred land.

Lips parted like oceans,
As I became forlorn,
And my gentle motion,
Made her waters drawn.

She was very restless,
Grasping into space,
As I laid gentle kiss,
Upon angelic face.

I applied the cuffs,
As her throat growled,
This was not enough,
She wanted me now.

My lover's deep moan,
Made it quite clear,
To sit upon her throne,
To be closer than near.

The chain became tight,
As the struggle began,
And I entered the tight,
Goddess's silk den.

A bite of soft lip,
As silk gate parted,
My shaft did slip,
As motion started.

Wearily she now rose,
And then fell upon me,
Her beautiful, exotic pose,
Completely shrouding me.

A hand on her thigh,
As I was buried in deep,
I slid my thumb inside,
Releasing goddess's weep.

Her eyes now met mine,
With thrust after thrust,
Our climax combined,
Soaked in our lust.

It just after four,
Now we were one,
Tolerating no more,
Gently I come.

We were no longer,
Restless.

PEAK

I wanna be within you,
When your silky waves crest,
Beads of my milky honeydew,
Burst and run into your nest.

Knuckles tighten with your grasp,
Muscles quaking in strong remorse,
Your voice straddles lusts deep gasp,
Heavenly bodies guide our course.

Waves surge and peak once more,
You shudder like the surf hitting land,
Clenched tight you release sacred door,
Releasing everything, but holding my hand.

BOUND

Bound and hog twined,
Maybe I am your guy,
If you have a wish to find,
Someone who likes to apply.

No need for the best,
Or sex from the host,
You want the hot mess,
Without ongoing boast.

Ideally you will choose,
With moistened fingertip,
He shall make me ooze,
Or he may make me rip.

It does not matter who,
Golden hot hard abs,
To take care of you,
Make you feel bad.

It's your wise choice,
A servant called man,
To lose your voice,
And rise within again.

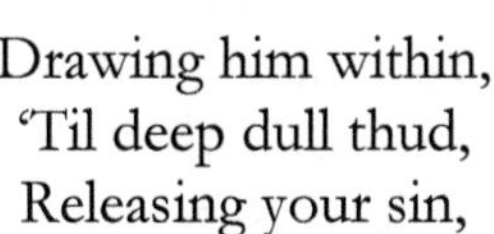

Drawing him within,
'Til deep dull thud,
Releasing your sin,
Scented in lust.

You curl up and pray,
Awaiting my palm sting,
Ecstatically we play,
Upon finish we begin.

I'd love you forever,
We'd sin all the seven,
Until you said never,
Souls bound toward heaven.

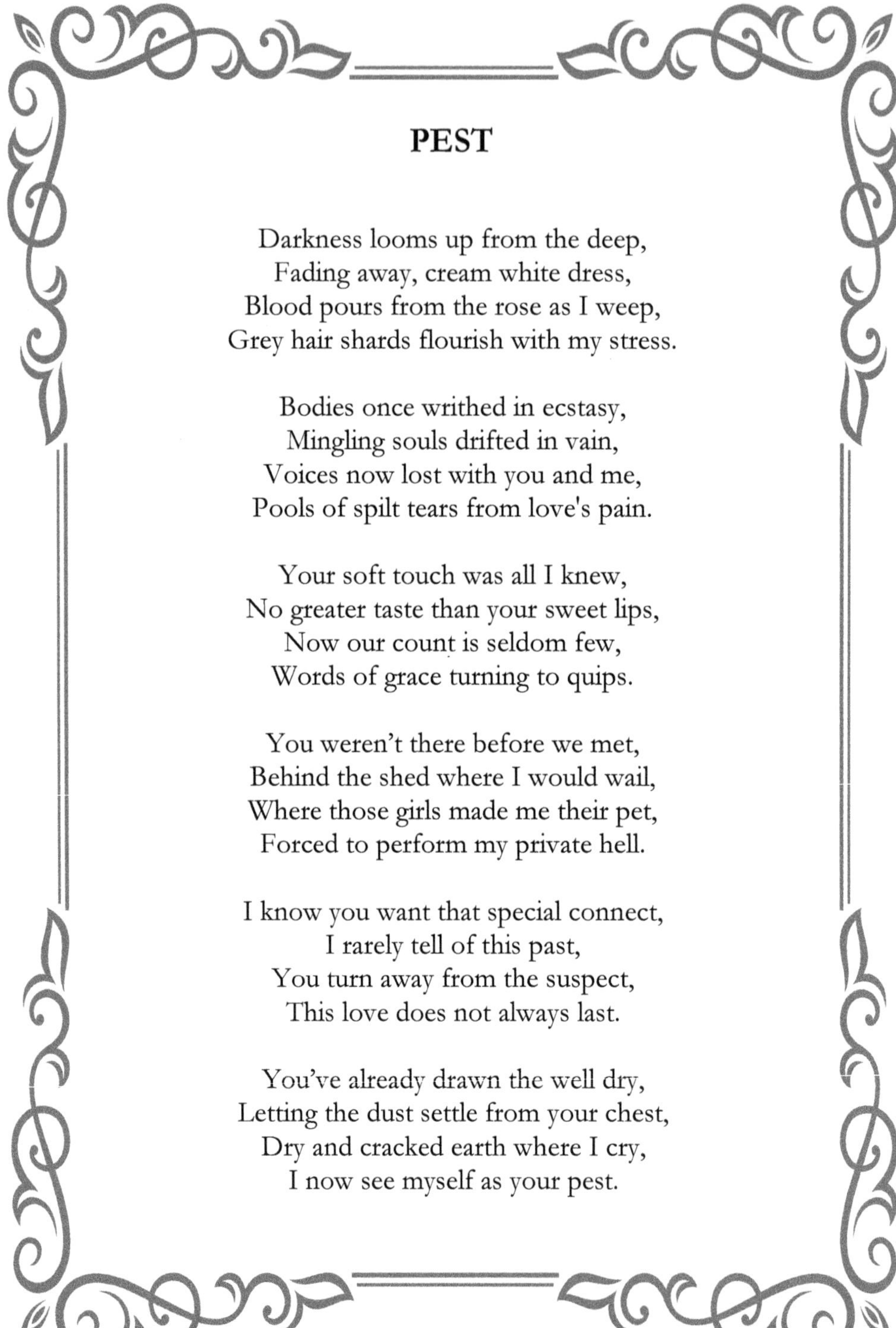

PEST

Darkness looms up from the deep,
Fading away, cream white dress,
Blood pours from the rose as I weep,
Grey hair shards flourish with my stress.

Bodies once writhed in ecstasy,
Mingling souls drifted in vain,
Voices now lost with you and me,
Pools of spilt tears from love's pain.

Your soft touch was all I knew,
No greater taste than your sweet lips,
Now our count is seldom few,
Words of grace turning to quips.

You weren't there before we met,
Behind the shed where I would wail,
Where those girls made me their pet,
Forced to perform my private hell.

I know you want that special connect,
I rarely tell of this past,
You turn away from the suspect,
This love does not always last.

You've already drawn the well dry,
Letting the dust settle from your chest,
Dry and cracked earth where I cry,
I now see myself as your pest.

BOUNTY

I roll, twisted and contorted,
Your taste residing in my mouth,
Dimensions are so distorted,
From the image of your soft pout.

Restless fantasy from pitch night,
Calm sieges my inner fears,
Words deliver me to my plight,
When used while you are near.

My hide seeks a passionate touch,
Like the rose that weathers a storm,
The searing heat hurts too much,
Sets my flight path away from norm.

The grounded jeer as I take wing,
While the clutch from our nest plays,
Shadows cry out as I now sing,
My soul spills out without delay.

Fearless eagle alone in flight,
Fragile shells crazed and cracked,
A path now set to my single sight,
A hunter's bounty must come back.

REACH

It feels just like a dream,
You are viewed but not seen,
Felt but never touched,
Observed and not judged.

Waking up does not appeal,
Unless it's to each other for real,
Where we walk upon a common land,
With your palm in my hand.

Would anyone else truly care,
About this infernal nightmare,
Chained to the devil's plight,
Lying awake throughout the night.

Life is too short to live without dreams,
So choose your beat or melody,
The strongest chains may be broke,
Weakened when you finally woke.

Our distant lives across the seas,
Reunited like a cool fresh breeze,
From past souls and forgotten past,
What once was one is no longer two halves.

Now you tremble about flight,
You shall glide to my side,
As the air of winged dove,
Drifts upon timeless love.

Footprints embedded in the sand,
Shadowed by hand in hand,
Framed by bodies side by side,
Devoid of turmoil deep inside.

It now seems so simple to see,
How you once belonged to me,
With sunken footprints upon the beach,
Your body and soul finally within my reach.

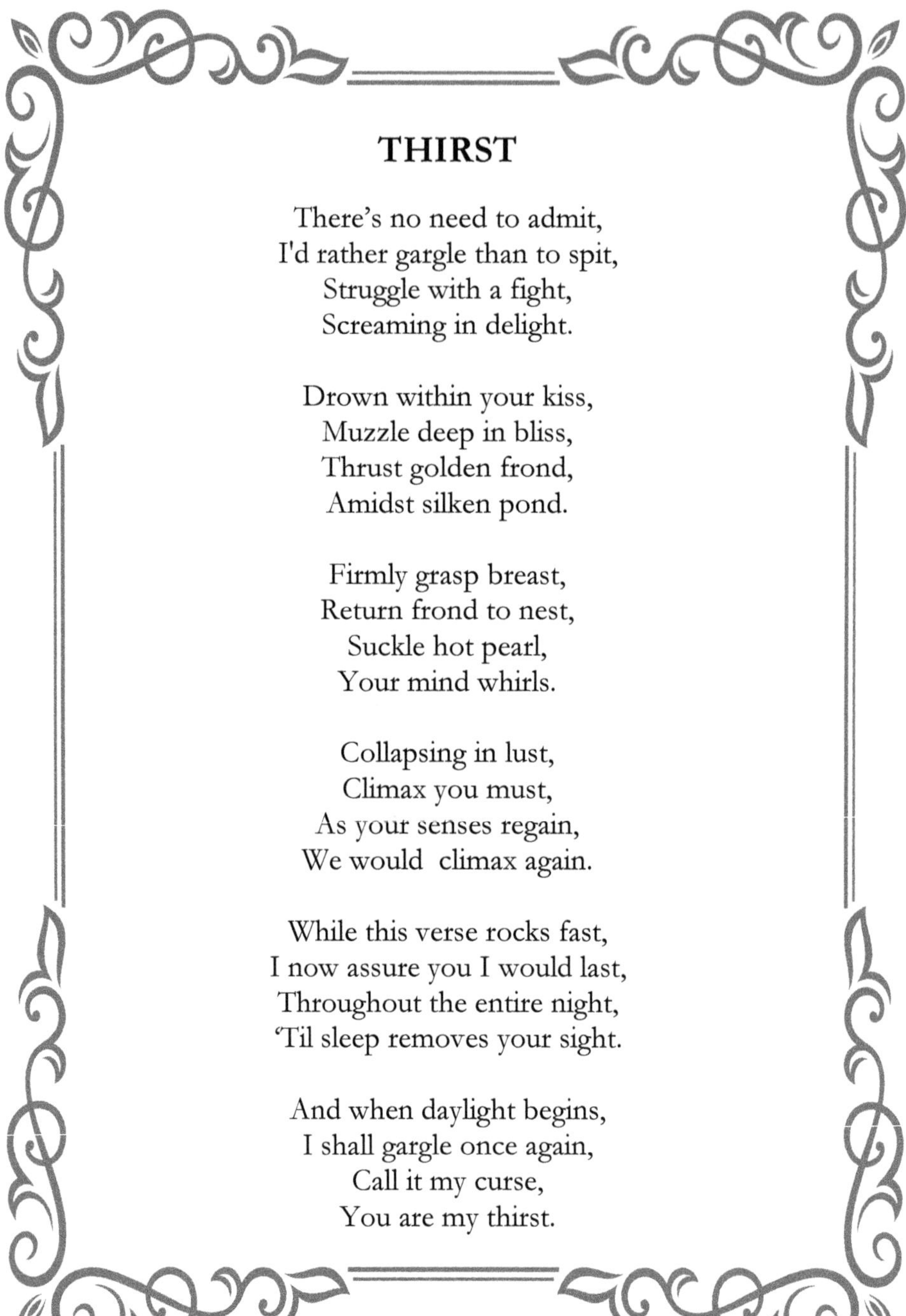

THIRST

There's no need to admit,
I'd rather gargle than to spit,
Struggle with a fight,
Screaming in delight.

Drown within your kiss,
Muzzle deep in bliss,
Thrust golden frond,
Amidst silken pond.

Firmly grasp breast,
Return frond to nest,
Suckle hot pearl,
Your mind whirls.

Collapsing in lust,
Climax you must,
As your senses regain,
We would climax again.

While this verse rocks fast,
I now assure you I would last,
Throughout the entire night,
'Til sleep removes your sight.

And when daylight begins,
I shall gargle once again,
Call it my curse,
You are my thirst.

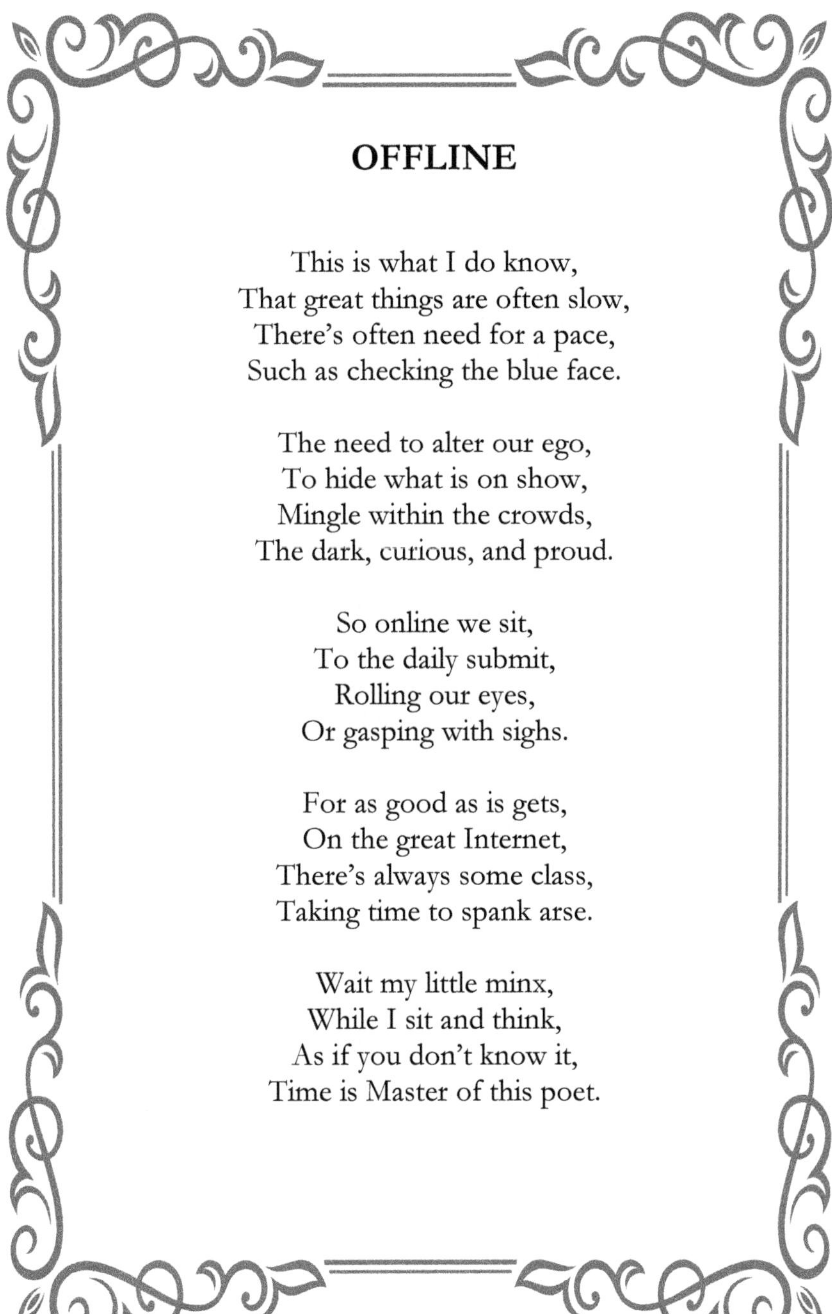

OFFLINE

This is what I do know,
That great things are often slow,
There's often need for a pace,
Such as checking the blue face.

The need to alter our ego,
To hide what is on show,
Mingle within the crowds,
The dark, curious, and proud.

So online we sit,
To the daily submit,
Rolling our eyes,
Or gasping with sighs.

For as good as is gets,
On the great Internet,
There's always some class,
Taking time to spank arse.

Wait my little minx,
While I sit and think,
As if you don't know it,
Time is Master of this poet.

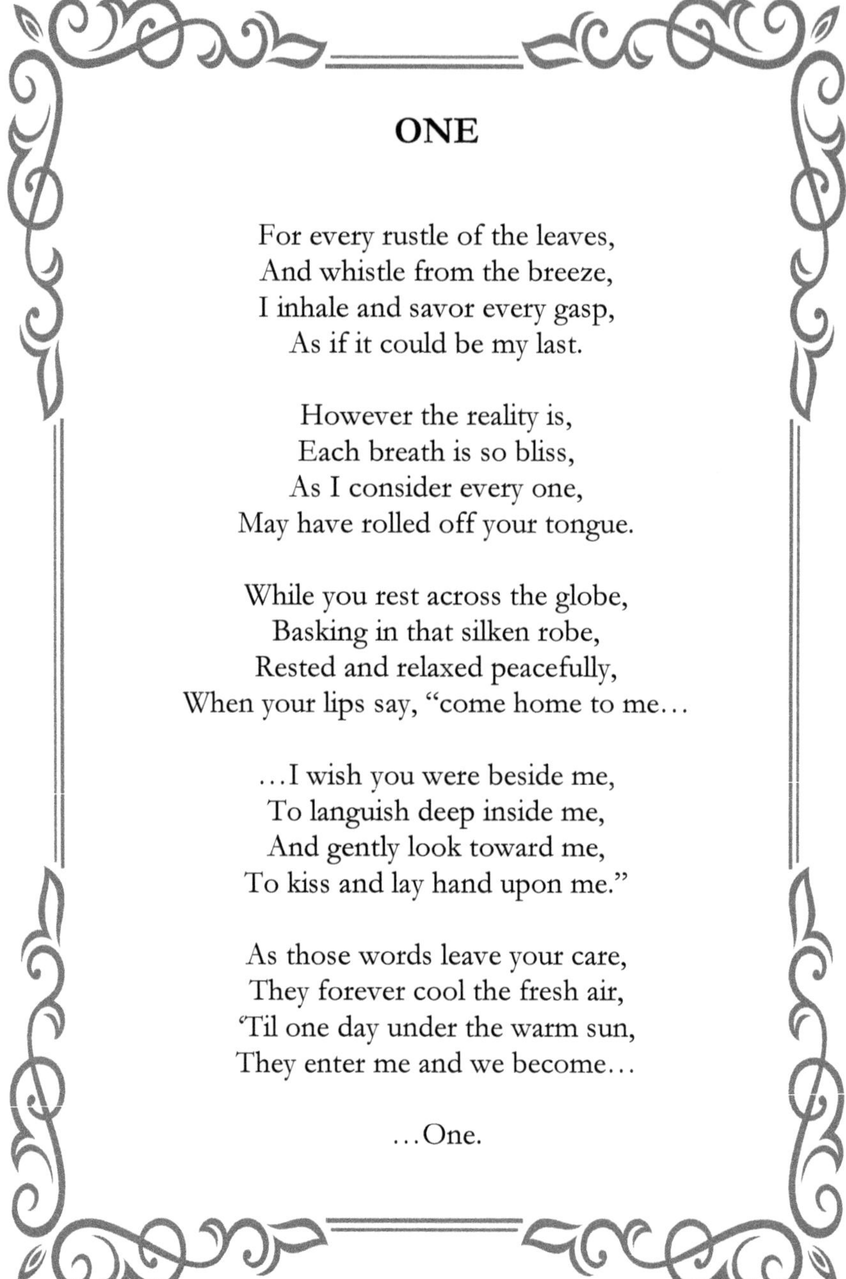

ONE

For every rustle of the leaves,
And whistle from the breeze,
I inhale and savor every gasp,
As if it could be my last.

However the reality is,
Each breath is so bliss,
As I consider every one,
May have rolled off your tongue.

While you rest across the globe,
Basking in that silken robe,
Rested and relaxed peacefully,
When your lips say, "come home to me…

…I wish you were beside me,
To languish deep inside me,
And gently look toward me,
To kiss and lay hand upon me."

As those words leave your care,
They forever cool the fresh air,
'Til one day under the warm sun,
They enter me and we become…

…One.

INTERNAL FLAME

I feel crowded when I am alone,
Lonely when you enter the room,
This fire burns deep inside of me,
A brand of passion you can't see.

Waters of lust may dampen the flame,
Quenching my thirst is not my game,
I have opened doors to wade into the deep,
My flame burns bright so long as you seek.

I'm just burning away while they condone,
No matter who I'm with or if I'm alone,
My flesh is my fare to the sodden earth,
My soul without you simply has no worth.

This is why I dread my daily slumber,
As you charge me with every stupid blunder,
Our vengeance is locked in two pairs of horns,
My patience and love is finally worn.

At night I lay back and emptily stare,
Soaking myself with a wall of tears,
Slowly they seep through my skin,
Damping the fire of passion within.

SLEEP FREAK

Like a surging torrent,
Bubbling up in the night,
I pry myself open,
And think to myself, right.

This cannot be happening,
I feel so fucking ill,
Am I destined to live,
At the mercy of these pills.

I tried to go natural,
And sleep through the night,
But here I am bundled,
Wound up all so tight.

Like a Vanilla soft swirl,
With a streak of freak,
Twisted and tormented,
Unable to speak.

I rush to the bottle,
And reach up to the shelf,
Opening the lid,
Seeking its help.

My little friend Blue,
One is often too much,
I pinch the fine line,
Into two halves I cut.

The fuckin' taste,
I hate it so bad,
I gulp it down in haste,
With a look so sad.

The freak in me,
Controls my own sleep,
Whether I do at all,
Shallow or deep.

BLUE TO BLACK

Ripped from my slumber & forced to take blue,
To see this night through,
Something on my chest,
I describe it as best.

To avoid taking a white,
I open screen basked in light,
It eases my sane,
Stops the shower of pain,
Sets me to ease,
Kills anxiety.

I rub one out,
Flowing in rhyme,
Before checking,
That friendly tweet line,
My heart stops pounding the beat,
Of a thousand drums,
Settles into a heap.

Sounding more like one,
Tempted,
Encouraged,
Inspired,
Wired.

Rest is no option,
My dreams almost forgotten,
Another blurt is required,
I'm the principle twist,
Flogged till open flesh,
By insomnia each night.

With my Parker beside me,
Not to write,
But to escape with me,
Back,
Into the black.

BURNING EMBER

Your startled nerves escape,
As the sense of fire emits,
A pinch across your nape,
While his finger gently flicks.

The burning from within,
As core of sacred ground,
Turns to amber sparks of sin,
Surge of mist settles upon mound.

An insatiable desire grows,
Darkness shatters upon ground,
Uncontrollable river flows,
Of lava surge without a sound.

World suddenly shrinks,
A scattering of clothing,
Fingers reach towards the brink,
Succumb to lust's loathing.

Charred from prior burns,
Hurt from the night before,
Lessons in love never learned,
One soul enters through the door.

Familiarity takes it shape,
As you dip and dive within,
No holding back the escape,
Of the scented gush of sin.

This journey is your own,
Aware of shortcuts at the pass,
As the ruler of your own throne,
You choose not to make it last.

Tension forced before relax,
Pumped with eager precision,
Shuddering instant climax,
As you pry open the incision.

PROPHESY

I'm a writer, not shipwrecked,
My letters won't be jammed in a bottle & tossed to sea.

You're a reader, not a beach,
Why risk the surf when you can follow me.

I'm a lover, not a leader,
My emotions swirl over and consummate me.

You're a spirit, not a vice,
Compulsion to live drives every need.

I'm a soul, not a being,
Never there but forever seen.

You're a beauty, not a disgrace,
Out of my sight is out of place.

I'm abundant in treasure,
Always there waiting when you seek luxury.

You're a fruit from the gods,
The thirst from your harvest, fulfills my prophecy.

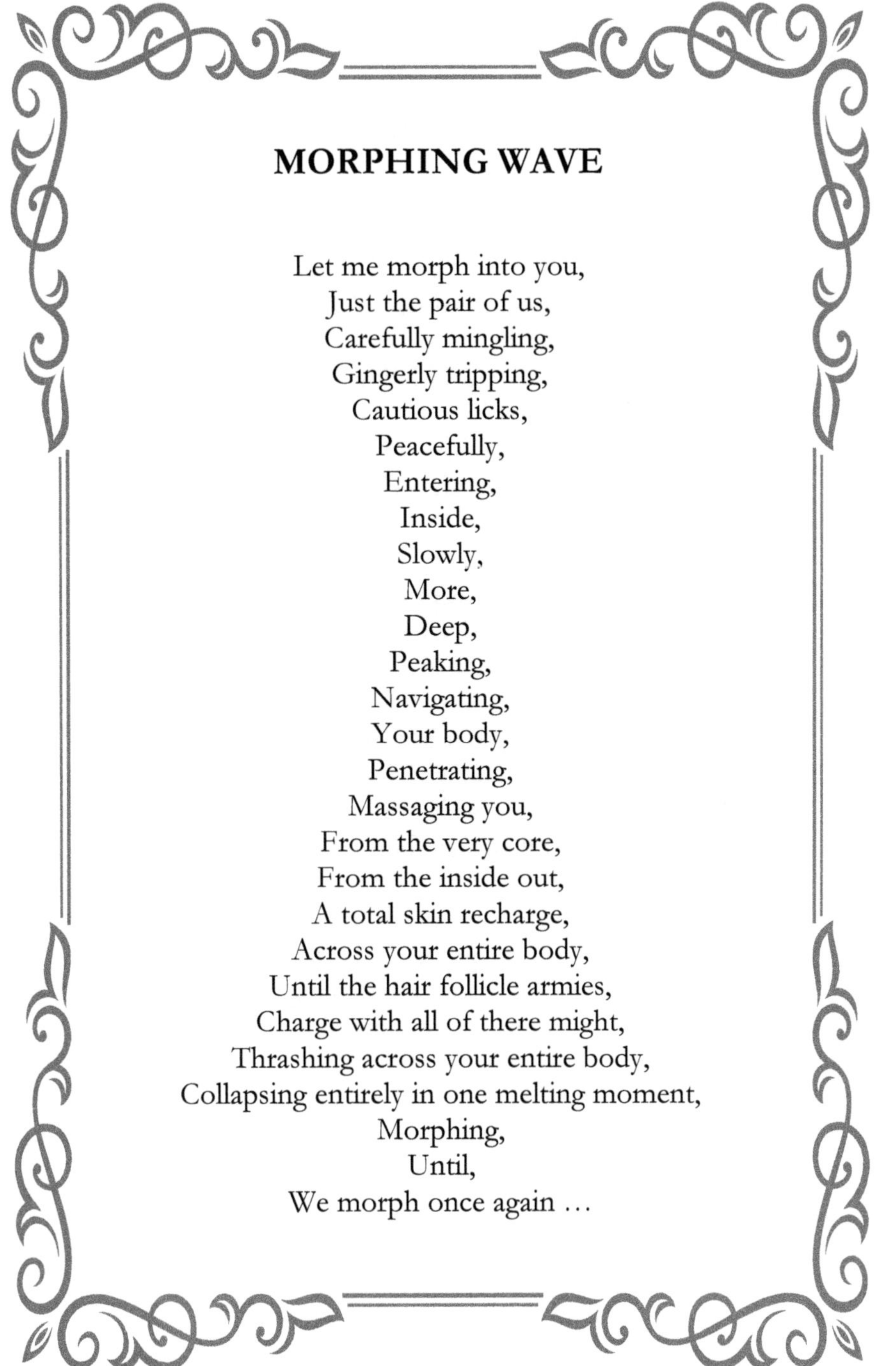

MORPHING WAVE

Let me morph into you,
Just the pair of us,
Carefully mingling,
Gingerly tripping,
Cautious licks,
Peacefully,
Entering,
Inside,
Slowly,
More,
Deep,
Peaking,
Navigating,
Your body,
Penetrating,
Massaging you,
From the very core,
From the inside out,
A total skin recharge,
Across your entire body,
Until the hair follicle armies,
Charge with all of there might,
Thrashing across your entire body,
Collapsing entirely in one melting moment,
Morphing,
Until,
We morph once again …

PRAYER FOR NEWTOWN

I'm barely up this morn,
When I'm told of several score,
Brought down without warn,
At the clutches of death's whore.

Yet another cold killing spree,
Brought to you by the "innocent kid",
One of our victims of this society,
A first-time offender who never hid.

We are all victims of the same gun,
The great invention of the human race,
As long as we share the same sun,
We will suffer the same fate.

We lose a dozen here and there,
Within the grounds where we learn rules,
It's really not as if nobody cares,
Yet under still swings their blood pools.

I'm fucked? Really? Can't you see?
Take a look what's going down around me,
Pint sized kids laughing, having fun,
At the whim of their friends, steaming blood runs.

We listen out for the bullets,
But by then it's way too late,
Now should we listen to cries,
Of their vengeance and hate.

I sit up, cry, and nearly hurl,
Full of lust and empty despair,
Admire my sleeping boys and girl,
Wishing their future full of love and care.

INSOMNIAC'S LAMENT

Tossing and turning,
Muscles are burning,
Confounded aching,
Absent lovemaking.

She blankets my thigh,
I emit a sleepy sigh,
My corpse within,
Carved through sin.

I scrape open the glass,
Where to write at last,
Peeling away the layers,
In this world of slayers,
Whose torment and virtue,
Shall not ever hurt you,
As the very wall protects,
From those who may wreck.

This silent household,
Where love now lies cold,
Is it asking too much,
To sooth through touch,
Where others cannot,
Yet, you choose to block,
Away my hunger and pain,
To where we once began.

So I shall rot further still,
To suckle the blue pill,
Letting my soul burn fast,
Making lost time go past,
Grieving insomniac lament,
Seizing my mind like cement.

DAM

Red to Black,
Tonight she returned,
What left me burnt,
That sharp little edge,
Where sleep is wedged,
Alert tension kicks in,
My precursor to sin.

Swallowing my daily intake,
Four pills make me quake,
Upon my back I rest,
What once was a nest,
Desperate, I try and fall,
Sleep doesn't come at all.

I'm caught between her teeth,
Grit rises from beneath,
Keeps me from sinking,
Silently I'm now thinking…

Dam.

I'm still awake,
Effects of the pill,
No longer a thrill,
Against Doctor's order,
More reds I slaughter,
Double the course,
To remove this remorse.

They ease the pain,
With minor touch of shame,
Still well beneath the dose,
But nothing to boast,
As the numbness kicks in,
Removing any urge to sin.

It's getting so late,
I'm left at the gate,
Effects are finally seen,
Shadow where I've been,
A drug induced delay,
Finally I'm getting away.

Dam.

I'm splitting,
Sounds now vibrate,
From what's on late
Feet shimmer in zing,
Toes can't feel a thing,
I'm now feeling sliced,
Like a rope un-spliced.

I down another pair,
No longer am I here,
I really wont be missed,
Blow me a goodbye kiss.

Dam.

I'm wasted,
Knees weighted with lead,
Body destined for bed,
Lost and scratching at door.

Room splits into two.
I'm caged in a zoo,
Shadows of beasts now stare,
My mind cannot repair,
Still throwing up a fight,
I chug down a white.

Zing now feels fine,
Washed with white wine,
Now come the quakes,
And my body now makes,
Dashes of blue light,
Crackling across fingers and eyes.

The zing now fills my girth,
Thrown for what I'm worth,
Barely able to lift limb,
Finally, sleep begins,
I float down to the floor,
Pinned down like a whore,
Doubling reds and adding white,
Finally takes this world, from my sight.

Dam,
I'm exhausted

PIECE OF ME

Insert a little piece of me,
Let me set your inhibitions free,
Unfold your wings as I tease,
Languishing in unbridled seas.

Stay with me as I gently ease,
Grasping me between your knees,
Let me swim through your seam,
Unlock your heart with my key.

Sparks of desire ignite lust sprees,
Writhe with me amidst your pleas,
With engorged clasp you shall seize,
Linger a little longer please.

Rocking slowly amidst the breeze,
Hold me in your arms & squeeze,
Take me complete tranquility,
Consume a little piece of me.

ENTRÉE

Threaded and stitched seams,
Glistening silver moonbeams,
Silent shadows within the dark,
Gentle beating of distilled heart.

Limbs rustle from under cover,
Glow of warmth from my lover,
Baptized through salty tears,
Amidst darkness she appears.

Embellished pain lying awake,
Aching limbs thrash as if innate,
Subdued mind at end of tether,
Discrete search for the leather.

Still dark air sliced to the quick,
Tarnished flesh rises from a whip,
Crop descends with a swift dance,
Partnered by passionate lance.

Moon light breeze induces quiver,
Ornate rope-work forms over liver,
Blood of lust now gushes to head,
Suspended within the tightened web.

Any creak from knotted rope,
Uncovers her passionate hope,
Fluid response to roaming finger,
Scent of her jewel begins to linger.

Rush of blood reveals her butterfly,
Tongue trickles slowly across thigh,
Across delicate wings toward her hood,
My palate suckling what it could.

SUMMER AIR

Sweet summer air,
Barely noticed you there,
'Til chill down my spine,
Our senses intertwine.

That sensual blast,
Forever may it last,
Neck to my hips,
Across sensitive lips.

Thirst consumes me,
Scent so heavenly,
Soul drawn to you,
Unsure what to do.

You detect my nerves,
Cautiously you observe,
Under taint of your eye,
I crumble between thighs.

We walk gentle pasture,
Your sun adorned posture,
Nothing on earth it seems,
Could further weaken my knees.

Drifting stride by stride,
Swimming with your tide,
We cast eye across the land,
Gently you grasp my hand.

As the sun settles above,
Peaceful as a white dove,
You become my only fare,
Amidst that sweet summer air.

DIVINE

Day falls down,
As night climbs high,
Tears form on cheek,
As you sigh.

Can’t love you more,
Yet I try,
A simple kiss,
Would make me fly.

I can't resist lust
Yet I must try,
Silent words,
Shall make me cry.

Shadowed touch,
Prompts a sigh,
I embrace true love,
While I lie.

Absent touch,
Prompts me to die,
Any desire,
Is second to mine.

We share ourselves,
In due time,
Our aching bodies,
Will intertwine.

The precious fruit,
From sacred vine,
Ripe and tender,
Taste so divine.

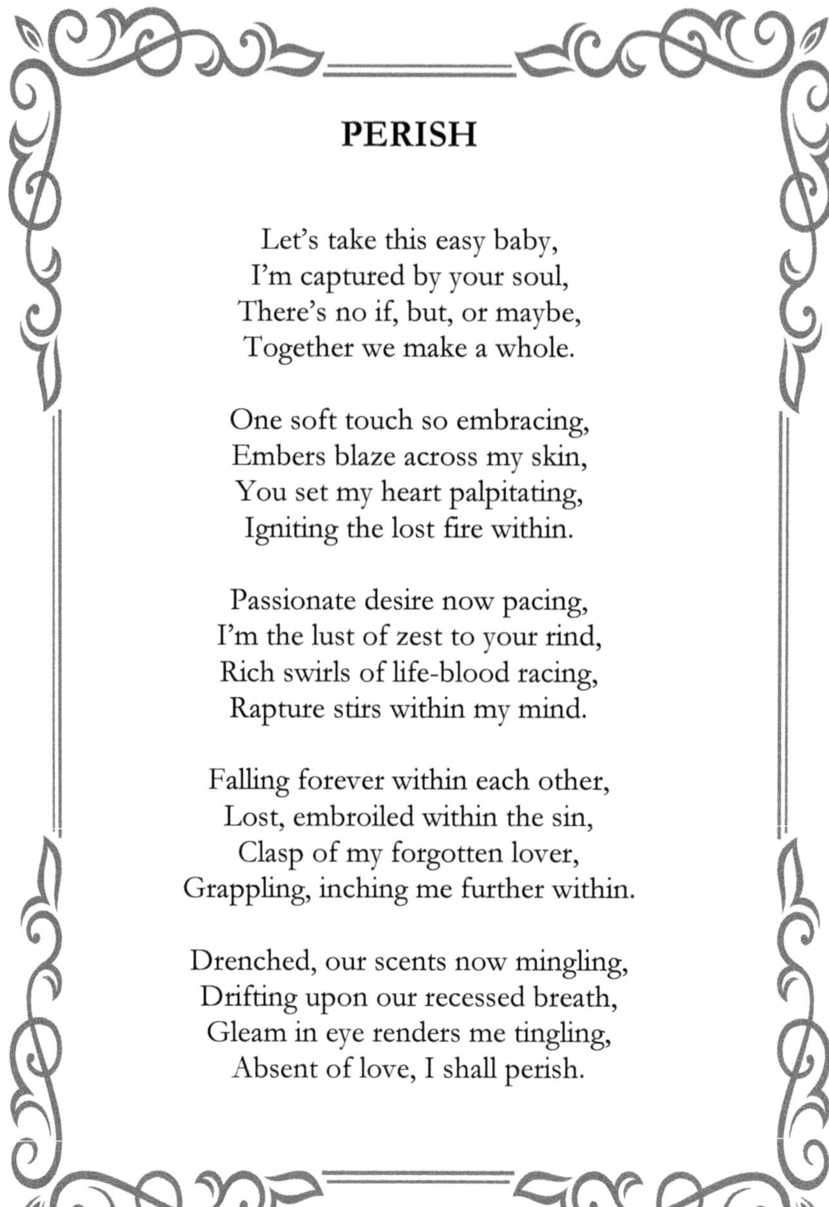

PERISH

Let's take this easy baby,
I'm captured by your soul,
There's no if, but, or maybe,
Together we make a whole.

One soft touch so embracing,
Embers blaze across my skin,
You set my heart palpitating,
Igniting the lost fire within.

Passionate desire now pacing,
I'm the lust of zest to your rind,
Rich swirls of life-blood racing,
Rapture stirs within my mind.

Falling forever within each other,
Lost, embroiled within the sin,
Clasp of my forgotten lover,
Grappling, inching me further within.

Drenched, our scents now mingling,
Drifting upon our recessed breath,
Gleam in eye renders me tingling,
Absent of love, I shall perish.

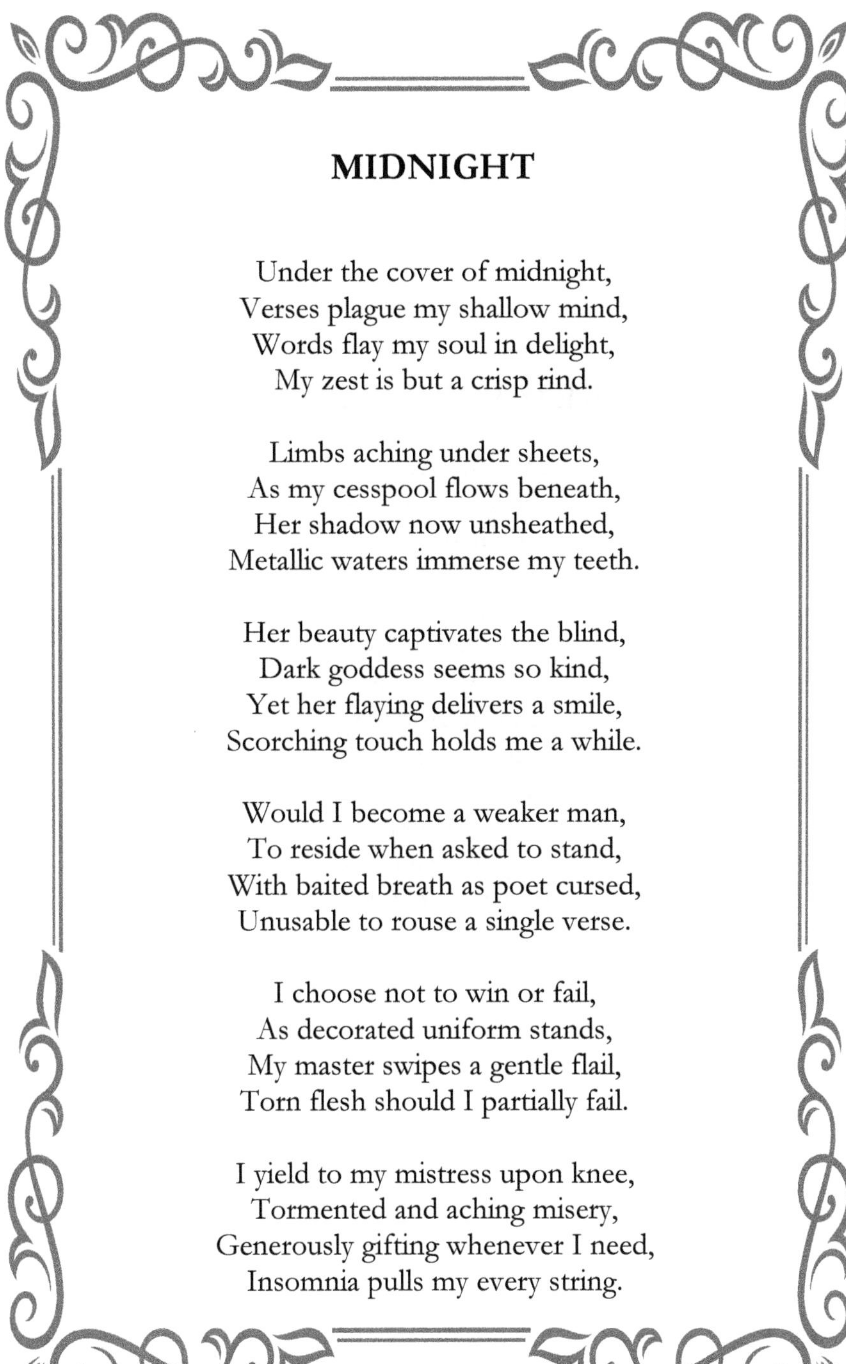

MIDNIGHT

Under the cover of midnight,
Verses plague my shallow mind,
Words flay my soul in delight,
My zest is but a crisp rind.

Limbs aching under sheets,
As my cesspool flows beneath,
Her shadow now unsheathed,
Metallic waters immerse my teeth.

Her beauty captivates the blind,
Dark goddess seems so kind,
Yet her flaying delivers a smile,
Scorching touch holds me a while.

Would I become a weaker man,
To reside when asked to stand,
With baited breath as poet cursed,
Unusable to rouse a single verse.

I choose not to win or fail,
As decorated uniform stands,
My master swipes a gentle flail,
Torn flesh should I partially fail.

I yield to my mistress upon knee,
Tormented and aching misery,
Generously gifting whenever I need,
Insomnia pulls my every string.

TREMBLING EARTH

Majestic creature,
Delicate features,
Radiant smile,
Elegant style,
Sensual sight,
Heartfelt delight,
Angelic face,
Tantric embrace,
Penetrating touch,
Embracing clutch,
Sensitive kiss,
Captivating bliss,
Pleasurable purse,
Trembling earth.

DELIGHT

Morning would be great,
But this future is my fate,
Bound within time & mist,
Musky scent feels so bliss.

I wear a pout upon my lips,
As we pass like floating ships,
Forever hidden within the night,
Yet never further than one's sight.

I am always held close to thee,
Yet restrained by depth of sea,
So each night I must reel,
As you become my last meal.

The thought of you and me,
Writhing in complete ecstasy,
Keeps me alive throughout the night,
Seeking pleasure; finding delight.

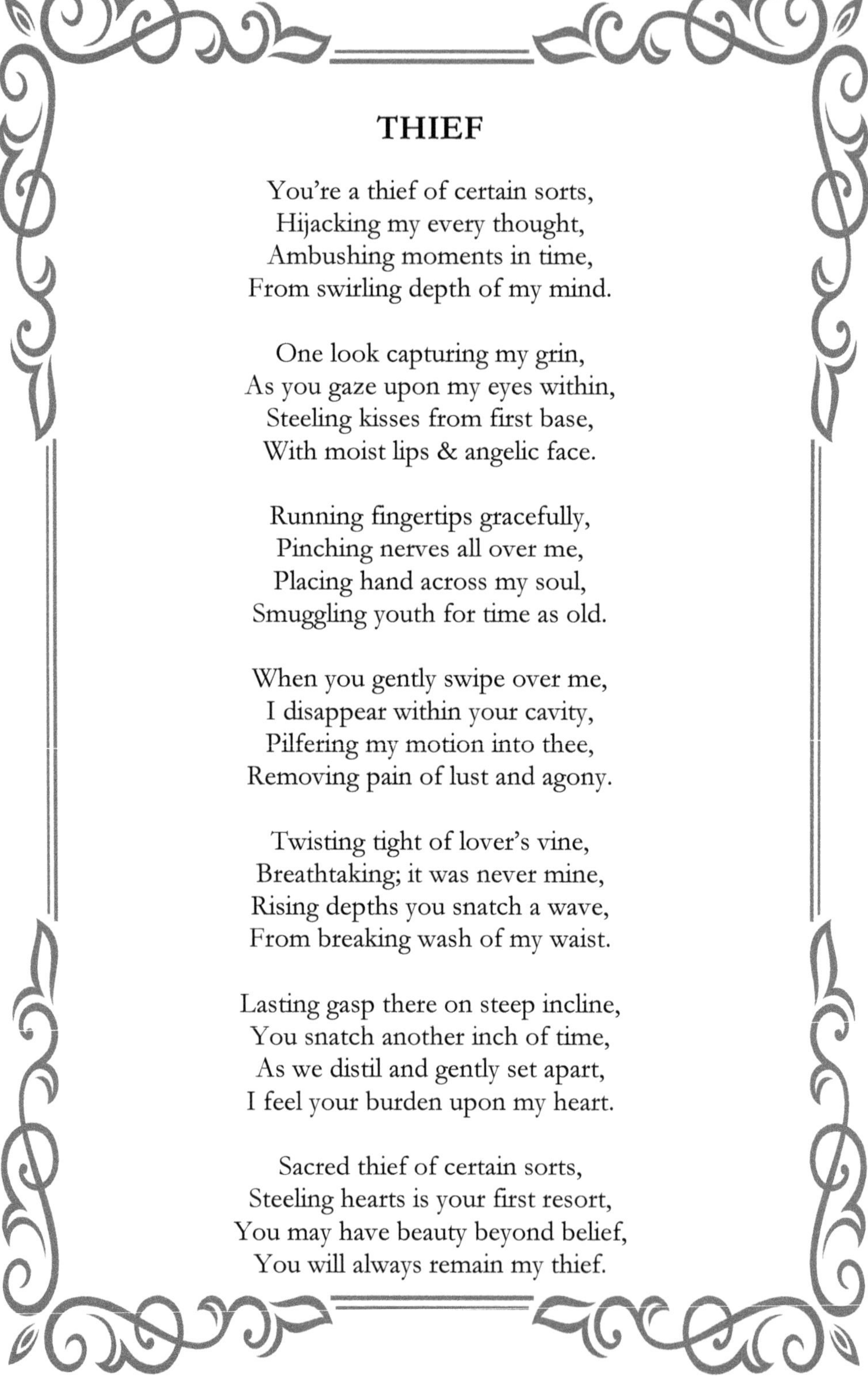

THIEF

You're a thief of certain sorts,
Hijacking my every thought,
Ambushing moments in time,
From swirling depth of my mind.

One look capturing my grin,
As you gaze upon my eyes within,
Steeling kisses from first base,
With moist lips & angelic face.

Running fingertips gracefully,
Pinching nerves all over me,
Placing hand across my soul,
Smuggling youth for time as old.

When you gently swipe over me,
I disappear within your cavity,
Pilfering my motion into thee,
Removing pain of lust and agony.

Twisting tight of lover's vine,
Breathtaking; it was never mine,
Rising depths you snatch a wave,
From breaking wash of my waist.

Lasting gasp there on steep incline,
You snatch another inch of time,
As we distil and gently set apart,
I feel your burden upon my heart.

Sacred thief of certain sorts,
Steeling hearts is your first resort,
You may have beauty beyond belief,
You will always remain my thief.

REALITY BITE

My fate is now done,
After three red & half one,
Blue to keep me true,
Yet still absent from you.

It's my own plight,
And something I daily fight,
The running sands of time,
Echoing in my rhymes.

Which only gets worse,
And I now edit my verse,
The glass tilted back,
To wash those demons back.

But it's so easy for me.
To see what I really see,
That I need to be complete,
For those that I treat.

In the hot beating sun,
From oldest to little one,
Where any absence of mind,
Would be most unkind.

Amidst these endless days,
I'm lost to the blue haze,
Of clear skies up above,
Playful giggles and their love.

Once again ships in sea,
Shall miss their destiny,
As all watching will soon see,
Deepest sleep becomes me.

Try as I might,
It's not anything I can fight,
This deep slumber at night,
Is now my reality bite.

MY CONSTELLATION

I want you to block out the moon,
And soar through the evening sky,
As you knit with me like a loom,
Suckling my essence,
'Til I am dry.

Break open my earth in lust,
While bearing down on my hips,
Incarnating my firm sex so deep,
Should my loving root,
Caress your moist lips.

Your passionate soul shall weep,
Flooding plains like genesis within,
Together tonight as we eclipse,
You become,
My constellation.

LOVE'S RETURN

Fate has swept me upon this beach,
Tossed from the surf of lover's breach,
Wasting away as faded driftwood,
Drowned in depth as only a lover could.

Sun beats mercilessly upon my hide,
Its energy pulls tears from my hide,
Withering to grey and brittle form,
Soul draining away to cold from warm.

Moistened only by tears,
Wakened by nightmares,
Waiting silently,
For love's return back to me.

SWIM WITH ME

Swim with me,
Through distant water to the sea.

Play melody,
Hum a lullaby as I gaze at thee.

Set me free,
Kiss my soft lips so sensitively.

Bake and kneed,
Work my dough thoughtfully.

Rise to me,
Alleviate while crouched on knee.

Sinfully,
Bathing within trickling stream.

Laboriously,
Vigorously plowing through silk seam.

Climatically,
Entrenched in you whole you scream.

Silently,
Heart beating as you now breathe.

Ecstasy,
Our bodies intertwine as we relieve.

HIS TOUCH

Mouth salivates,
Body now levitates,
Heat surging in the night,
Soul prepped to take flight,
My flesh is longing to turn,
Forbidden urges to churn,
Seeking forbidden pleasure,
Demanding his measure,
Soaked so deep within,
The original deadly sin,
Kneeling to ground,
Make no sound,
I'm awaiting,
His touch.

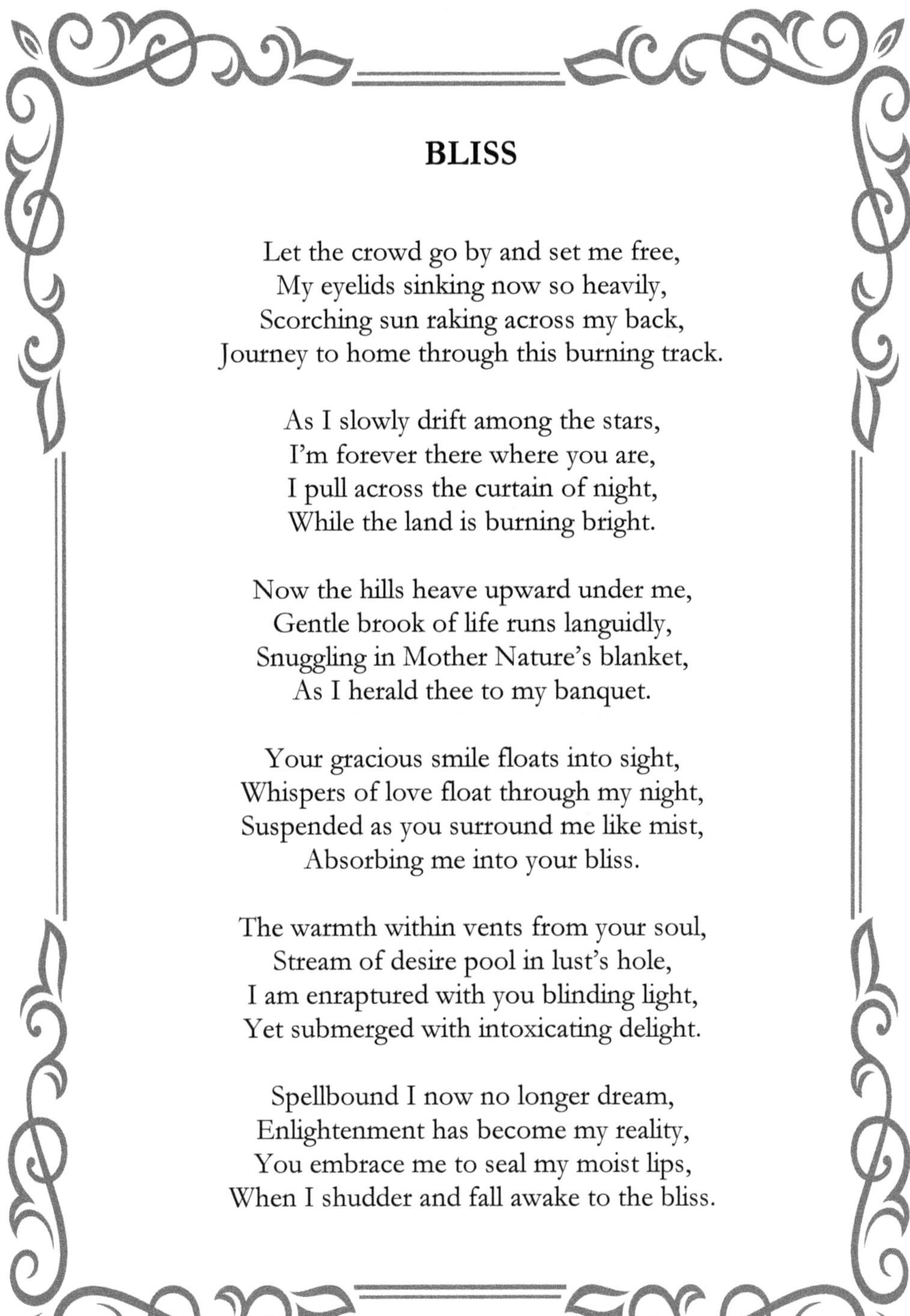

BLISS

Let the crowd go by and set me free,
My eyelids sinking now so heavily,
Scorching sun raking across my back,
Journey to home through this burning track.

As I slowly drift among the stars,
I'm forever there where you are,
I pull across the curtain of night,
While the land is burning bright.

Now the hills heave upward under me,
Gentle brook of life runs languidly,
Snuggling in Mother Nature's blanket,
As I herald thee to my banquet.

Your gracious smile floats into sight,
Whispers of love float through my night,
Suspended as you surround me like mist,
Absorbing me into your bliss.

The warmth within vents from your soul,
Stream of desire pool in lust's hole,
I am enraptured with you blinding light,
Yet submerged with intoxicating delight.

Spellbound I now no longer dream,
Enlightenment has become my reality,
You embrace me to seal my moist lips,
When I shudder and fall awake to the bliss.

IF ONLY

If only I could show you,
How much I want you.

If only I could pull you inside of me,
To let you see through my eyes,
Feel the beating of my heart,
How it surges with desire for you.

If only you could tremble & quake,
Like the thunder and rain,
As my dammed passion bursts,
Washing our souls away.

If only you could feel the breeze,
As my breath falls upon your neck,
While we float away,
Amidst the clouds within our dreams.

If only I could show you
How much I love you.

UNDER COVER

Once again I lament,
Thrashing about in cement,
Verses swirl in my head,
Amidst the blue and red.

The scorching heat,
From your body greets,
Me under the cover,
Satiated lover.

My head toppling to stop,
The torment in my dreams,
I would quite prefer other,
Pop a white after the other.

As I float in the rich ambience,
My wait for sleep tests patience,
'Til thoughts of my precious lover,
Silently swells under my cover.

I GOT A THING

I got a thing for you and me,
Washing my beach like the sea,
Cradled within velvet luxury,
We embrace so passionately.

Absorb my pressure as you ease,
Shroud me in darkness so deep,
Drifting together now elegantly,
Clasping tight as you seep.

Nothing moves so beautifully,
Not even stars and galaxies,
I embrace while you are trembling,
I got a thing for you this love we keep.

REMEMBER

Could you recall a better time?
When laughter spilt like red wine,
The flowers bloomed on our table,
Holding each other whenever able.

Could you imagine better days?
Rolling amidst summer hay,
Gentle kisses upon the beach,
Never being too far from reach.

Would you relive those late nights?
Your eyes lighting up upon sight,
Midnight air thick with romance,
Heels softly clicked as we danced.

Can you remember all the gifts?
If they were received with a kiss,
Were they ever your most wanted,
Or even make your heart grow fonder.

Will you remember times of love?
When neither could give enough,
Frantic pleasure amidst the zest,
When every time became the best.

Will you remember days of past?
When our love will forever last,
Cherished moments when we're old,
Our souls warmed up from bitter cold.

DESPAIR

There's a static charge in the air,
You're overcome with despair,
Present yourself to me tonight,
May you collapse through delight.

For eons, we have been apart,
Yet shared a love within our heart,
You waited for me so patiently,
Hollow chamber filled with agony.

Past mortal lives hath turned cold,
Though our love remains bold,
Now we catch the sand of time,
Eternally yours as you are mine.

Reunited with my one treasure,
Delicate body my guilty pleasure,
Immersed within luscious bath,
Caressing me until I am hard.

Drawing me where waters seep,
I plunge within towards the deep,
Rising up you stretch my sin,
Ensuring I'm thrust forth within.

Collapsing gently rises the tide,
As your hips provide my guide,
I'm sinking entirely into the depth,
My chiseled girth drives you inept.

I reside strong within my maiden,
Your tormented soul now fading,
Consuming every firm inch I bare,
Shuddering now in silent despair.

PLEASURE

In the pitch of the night,
From corner of my eye,
A heavenly delight,
She raises a brow,
What shall I do now,
There's only one thing,
I must hear her sing,
In orgasmic,
Ecstasy.

Seated upon leather,
Expecting pleasure,
Seductive bent hips,
Moist luscious lips,
Beckoning my touch,
Seated upon couch,
I must taste her seam,
In sensual,
Pleasure.

PRIMAL FEAR

Primal fear was once your foe,
You were too afraid to let go,
You feel as if you are alone,
It leaves you chilled to the bone.

He used to watch you fall,
That is why you built your wall,
Always running away to hide,
Or bottling it all up deep inside.

Until death shall do us apart,
Signed across your breaking heart,
Was all of that just in vain,
Would death had be an easier pain.

Glistening stars way up high,
Shine in teardrops from your eye,
What once echoed in beach shell,
Is now heard when my arms wrap round.

QUENCH

Tease me tenderly tonight,
Do the wrong that feels so right,
I vow I will not place myself first,
As I shall dine from your silk purse.

Nibble upon my moist bottom lip,
Present yourself so I may sip,
Guide my tongue within your seam,
Embrace me as I raise my beam.

Touch me with your fingers now,
Run them up and down my bow,
Engorged I offer my sacred trust,
Feast with me upon our lust.

Take the length of me right in,

And when you can no longer burden,
Quench my thirst from your moist curtain.

ECSTASY

Today I vow to take us places never before seen,
Amidst blurry mists of lust hidden deep within your dreams,
I propose this meeting time insisting you must attend,
Drinking from your glass of wine, lust's intoxicating blend.

My eyes have been upon you thinking of this night to come,
As I wait with great fortitude growing pain that shall be undone,
Now you arrive at end of day I peer from out of the blinds,
Retreating to where you may capture me for our first time.

Rose petals upon the stair a path to where I'll be found,
Scented mist drifts on the air you track me like lust's hound,
My voice rings out beckoning through the distilled night air,
You enter where I'm showering just watching me in the bare.

Foamy suds are now inciting thoughts of us within your mind,
Sight of my flesh igniting sexual desire of every kind,
Rolls of foam pour over me as you silently watch and admire,
All the while still not noticing Goddess's thirst for the fire.

Entering through the thick steam to grasp my strong wet hand,
Compelled to play out this dream and navigate my firm land,
Gently touching with your zest controlling your own fate,
Kneeling down as if to confess with my sex against your plate.

Amidst the water we pretend to be long lost distant lovers,
The sensations my firm flesh sends eases your moist cover,
Pressing digits deep into your sin realizing what you must,
Primed so fortuitously you begin to accept a need for my lust.

My fingers entangled in your hair I raise you to your feet,
Sealing your gasp with great care as our moist lips meet,
Grasping your gorgeous breast with hand across your pass,
Fingers curling into your crest touching you at long last.

Compelled to straddle my waist as I take hold of your hips,
Not afraid of my white paste, I ease my sex through your lips,
Steamy water within the shower now quickly begins to boil,
Splashes of raw sexual power our bodies start to recoil.

Senses lost within the rain as my sex heaves to and fro,
Almost reeling in the pain yet prepared to absorb my glow,
Our bodies are forced to comply while minds enforce the plunder,
Lusts descent cause us to fly as together we groan like thunder.

With remorse you shelter me while weakness comes to knees,
Embracing every inch as we rest our tantric souls to please,
Distant waves echo within as our minds envelop fantasy,
Consumed by our tantric orgasm we finally succumb to ecstasy.

SUBMISSION

Your presence flickers in the distance,
My soul prepares for zero resistance,
At your command, you are my host,
I am your sub chained to your post.

Your eyes capture me & penetrate within,
My goddess surges to rinse my sin,
Aching with lust, gently slipping away,
I remain paralyzed under your gaze.

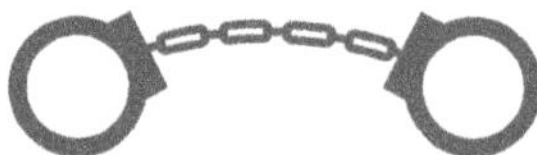

Your footsteps approach amidst the dark,
My ears ring with tones from a harp,
Beating within, my heart skips a beat
I kneel down to the shadow of your feet.

Your fingers pan out to offer a soft touch,
My flesh chills with shivers on its crust,
Trembling now, yet yearning to clasp,
I become soft putty within your grasp.

Your voice now commands me by name,
My lust melts like a candle to a flame,
Scintillating heat, burning with fear,
I comply to your words that I now hear.

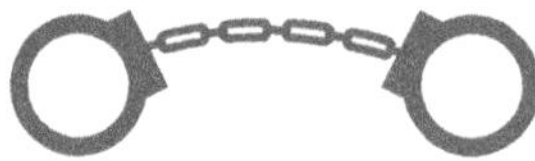

Your hand upon me enrages the fire,
My thighs ache with burning desire,
Lava churning, now rising to flush,
I silently beckon my waters to gush.

Your fingers unravel prior to furl,
My wings splay open with a twirl,
Slowly dancing, held by your musk,
I flood to saturate my dry husk.

Your motion brings me to the brink,
My mind is soon unable to think,
Waters rising, push becomes shove,
I encase you like a hand in a glove.

Your girth ruptures my love seam,
My tide rises from depths unseen,
Gently bathing, our bodies awash,
I utter praise of "oh my gosh".

ETERNAL FLAME

Have I found my lost romance,
Amidst a dream where we dance,
Our souls parted by eternity,
Bygone lust from history.

Our entwined flames meet at last,
Like a sea breeze at the pass,
Drifting upon my deep voice,
Across your skin soft and moist.

Kissing before the sun sets,
Majestic mist soaks you wet,
Embracing you with my arms,
Where his love will do no harm.

White wine in crystal glass,
A moment that will always last,
When out eyes finally met,
Like an angel heaven sent.

Our bodies writhe under sheets,
Icy breeze tickling our feet,
Sudden urge to kiss those lips,
Before transpiring to your hips.

Your essence on my palette,
A slip of lover's turrets,
Tongue probes deep in your sex,
Composure seems so complex.

Waters seeping from within,
Passionate fountain of your sin,
As you suckle my hardening vine,
Head to toe feels oh so divine.

With imminent release closing in at last,
You become the lost ship to my heavy mast,
Cloaked with passion as my shoulders lift,
Kindred souls intoxicated upon Aphrodite's spirits.

Fully engorged as we sail your playful seas,
Casting off ship's dock, I lower myself so gently,
Waves fall upon beach as I fill you to the brim,
Warm eddies mingle to release lust nymphs within.

Such an exquisite feeling as I slide from the dock,
An amorous storm wave washes over my cock,
I capture a breath to set sail from your lips,
Hugging the ocean as I grind against your hips.

Our slow rhythm gives way to waves of passion,
Rapids cresting from her lust as you imagine,
The climatic massaging of her internal skin,
And sensation of my hot seed released within.

The storm front breaks free,
Tossing us in ecstatic sea,
Now sailing so freely,
Struggling to breathe.

You gasp without fear,
Releasing divine tear,
So close and so near,
Both complete and bare.

You clasp and then release me,
Clasp and then release,
Clasp and release,
Clasp.

Blissfully.
Passionately.
Climatically.
Intensely.

Paused to take breath,
Once again before rest,
Burning embers from my vein,
Pouring over my eternal flame.

VELVET SEA

You are the bite welt upon my neck;
Laid upon me in a moment of divine insanity,
When your muscles ached from resolution,
And searing hot nails bit into my flesh,
Like an angel falling from the heavens above.

As you gently unravel,
I muzzle into your scented husk,
To feast unremorsefully upon life's nectar,
Until I unlock the translucent plains of lust,
And you immerse me in the velvet sea.

BURNING ANGEL

Scorched hearts blackened through pain,
Burning alive through tears of acid rain,
Volcano simmering deep underneath,
Separated in love by a single belief.

His sturdy frame and steady hand,
Shadow cast upon a distant land,
Her world of chaos and dreams,
Compels her into shadows unseen.

Worthless souls standing nearby,
Neither see or hear the Angel's cry,
Incapable of accepting their plight,
Igniting the fate of destiny's flight.

Water through time may erode any rock,
But nothing on earth governs the flock,
Rain or storm never drenches the wing,
Of lost souls that are prepared to dream.

Dusk blows away from their feet,
As air fills wing upon the breeze,
Gliding forever to those who care,
A flight of love for few that dare.

From a distance it becomes so clear,
Scorched hearts were always there,
The land was barren with burnt earth,
Torched by souls carrying no worth.

Two shadows drifted over the sea,
One filled of fate, the other destiny,
No penetrating beam could possibly light,
Shadows from hearts soaring in flight.

Within misty grey clouds two Angels meet,
Upon sight their hearts skip a beat,
Internal fires ignite upon single touch,
Fuelled by passion while drenched in lust.

Drifting upon the wind far above,
Reunited souls blazing with lost love,
Embracing one another within the mist,
Being held by an Angel is divine bliss.

His rippling torso and burning skin,
Enrapture flooding her sacred sin,
Two shadows entwine to become one,
Ablaze with heat that melts the sun.

Her search for love and desire complete,
Filled to the brim with his firm meat,
His soul sizzling under her hot mantel,
As she consumes her Burning Angel.

I MISS YOU

I see you,
& read you.

But I cannot,
Touch you,
Hear you,
Taste you,
Smell you,
Embrace you,
Be in you.

So,
I miss you.

ABOUT THE AUTHOR

PJ Bayliss lives in New Zealand where he writes poetry and stories as a casual hobby and form of relaxation. He is currently working on a romance novel series under the "Chemical Romance" title.

He works as a professional business consultant and has worked for several international organizations at home and abroad.

Learn more about him and his writing projects at:
www.pjbayliss.com

www.ingramcontent.com/pod-product-compliance
Ingram Content Group UK Ltd.
Pitfield, Milton Keynes, MK11 3LW, UK
UKHW051126260726
13967UKWH00010B/2896

9 780994 109002